FORD TRANSCONTINENTAL

at work

Patrick W Dyer

Old Pond
PUBLISHING LTD

ACKNOWLEDGEMENTS

My grateful thanks to the following for their help and support: John Nevill, Kelvin Brown, Martin Cottenden, Ian Walker, George Bennett, John W Henderson, Adrian Cypher, Marcus Lester, Clive Davis, David Wakefield, Del Roll, Kevin Walker, Dave Hill, Maurice Richardson, Brian Clemens, Alan Parr, Stephen Elford, Baden Chawkley and the Pie & Pint club, John Comer, Gordon Green, Philippe Brossette, Anne Carriere, all at Old Pond, and of course, Linda and Jess Dyer.

ABOUT THE AUTHOR

Patrick Dyer, born in 1968, grew up during one of the most notable and exciting periods of development for heavy trucks and also the last of the real glory days for trucking as an industry. This is reflected in his subject matter. His previous books covered the F88 and F89 from Volvo, the LB110, 111, 140 and 141 from Scania and the 2800, 3300 and 3600 from DAF. *Ford Transcontinental at Work* is Patrick's fifth book.

Although Patrick's day job is in motor sport, he holds a Class One licence and drives whenever the opportunity arises. He is also the proud owner of a 1983 Volvo F12, finished in the livery of Edwin Shirley Trucking, which he restored with the help of long-term friend, Ashley Pearce.

DECLARATION

There were at least six recognised methods of measuring engine output for trucks during the period covered by this book. Manufacturers and magazines often quoted different outputs for the same engine using BS.Au, SAE, DIN and ISO systems, some gross and some net, much to everyone's confusion. Therefore, for clarity, only the figures quoted by Ford at the time are used throughout this work.

DEDICATION

This book is dedicated to all those individuals, especially the hardcore ones that reside in and around Essex, who were involved in the concept, design and manufacture of the Transcontinental, one of the true icons of twentieth-century road haulage. We salute you.

First published 2012

Copyright © Patrick W Dyer, 2012

Patrick W Dyer has asserted his right under the Copyright, Designs and Patents Act, 1988, to be identified as the Author of this Work

ISBN 978-1-908397-10-2

A catalogue record for this book is available from the British Library

Published by
Old Pond Publishing Ltd
Dencora Business Centre,
36 White House Road
Ipswich IP1 5LT United Kingdom

www.oldpond.com

Front cover photograph
NWC 67V, a star of the Transcontinental PR fleet, poses at North Weald Aerodrome in early 1981 during a photo shoot organised in conjunction with *Truck* magazine, which was evaluating the truck at 38 tonnes prior to the increase in weight limits in 1983. *Truck* made regular use of the aerodrome as a photo location as it was conveniently located just a short distance up the M11 from its London office. *(Photo: Ford Motor Company)*

Back cover photograph
Sunderland-based Vaux Breweries put this handsome combination to work on its bulk beer deliveries handling Lorimers Best Scotch Ale, brewed in Edinburgh, and Samson bitter. Note the ingenious, rotating headlight wiper fitted to the outer units. *(Photo: Ford Motor Company)*

Cover design and book layout by Liz Whatling
Printed and bound in China

Contents

Foreword

By George Bennett
Editor, Truck magazine 1987-89 & 1990-97

Ford's legendary Transcontinental was one of the great nearly trucks. It did nearly everything right, and enthused nearly enough people to make it a profitable proposition for Ford. Patrick points out in this book that if buying decisions had been left to 10-year-old boys, the Transconti would have been a roaring success. That would have been just as true if decisions had been left solely to drivers, for the big Ford was a magnificent truck to drive. Regular users loved the high seating position, with its unrivalled visibility and potential for looking down on every other road user, they appreciated the slick Eaton-Fuller gearbox – at least in Britain where constant-mesh boxes were still the norm in the 1970s – and they relished the high-spec cab. Unfortunately, the Transconti had to earn money, and here the early versions gained a poor reputation that Ford never successfully dispelled.

My first experience of a Transconti was at Abbey Hill Group, based in Yeovil, in late 1975. The company had taken an early demonstrator for a week, and for a couple of days I was its driver. Coming from a ground-hugging AEC Mandator, I was almost suffering from vertigo by the time I'd climbed into the big Ford, but it was a wonderful truck to drive. Its only drawback was the four-point cab suspension, which was far softer than anything else on the road at the time, making the cab lurch and roll more than any truck I'd driven before.

Abbey Hill, which was then becoming a specialist car transport firm, had no intention of buying a truck that clearly had no future as a car transporter, and we drivers weren't even asked our opinion, but when I moved to Williams Transport in Porthmadog, North Wales, it was a different matter. Here the small company tried a number of demonstrators in earnest, and I was given every one of them for assessment.

When a Transcontinental arrived, we drivers were very excited, because our firm also had a Ford car dealership, and we'd heard that would mean a hefty dealer discount on the Transconti. Although we never paid much attention to fuel economy in those days, I carefully monitored the Ford's fuel figures. They were hardly impressive, but it wasn't miles per gallon that killed the deal, it was unladen weight.

I clearly remember my first run in the Ford, driving through Snowdonia and on to Atherstone in Warwickshire, hauling a flat trailer loaded with cheese. On the narrow, winding roads of North Wales, the cab lean took some getting used to, but the view was magnificent. I'd heard that some Scania was 'King of the Road', but as far as I was concerned, the Transconti claimed its throne. I was very familiar with the Fuller box – I drove one every day in my Scammell Crusader – and the Ford's was a light and slick installation.

I happily imagined myself driving the Transconti every day, until I went for the backload. Here my daydream evaporated, because the Ford was so heavy that I had to load two fewer pallets – amounting to two tons less – than I could put behind the Crusader. I might have loved the Transconti as a driver, but I couldn't recommend a truck that might knock 10 per cent off the revenue from every load. With a heavy heart I reported back to the office, and that was the end of my Transconti dream.

Some years later, when I was researching an article on the Transconti for a pilot edition of *Truck & Driver* magazine, I verified that Ford had shed a considerable amount of weight from the early versions, as Patrick explains in Chapter Two. When *Truck* magazine tested the Transconti in 1975, it weighed 7,400 kg, but four years later the vehicle was slimmed down to a more competitive 7,000 kg. Had Ford managed the weight savings from the start, the Transconti story might have been rather different, and I might have even have ended up driving one full time.

For the same article, I also talked to a senior Ford engineer, who told me that in the very early stages of the project, Ford had considered major components that would have made its flagship a very different beast, including a Mercedes engine, a ZF gearbox and a DAF cab. In the event, as Patrick explains, Ford went for the Cummins/Fuller/Rockwell driveline that the company understood so well from its US experience, and the Berliet cab that established the Transconti's classy image.

As a driver, my later experience of the Transcontinental was mainly when running to the Middle East with other drivers. On my very first trip I fell in with two brothers who drove for Hicks of Rhiwderin in South Wales. One drove a Transconti and the other a recently introduced 'New Generation' Mercedes; there was no question which brother was the happier with his truck, and of course it was the roomy Ford that had enough space for several drivers to socialise together.

In the Middle East I discovered the oddity that faced all Transcontinental drivers, which Patrick refers to in the caption accompanying the picture of Birdale International's Transconti, on page 42. Since 1966, Arab countries had operated a boycott against several major US companies, including Coca Cola and Ford. The Ford boycott was the result of a licensing agreement between Ford and an Israeli firm, to assemble British and American Ford trucks and tractors for the Israeli market, and its effect was to ban Fords from all Arab countries.

Transcontinental drivers and operators got round this by listing their trucks as Berliets or Cummins, and by stripping the trucks of their Ford badging themselves. I remember a couple of early Transcontis which had the FORD letters across the front rearranged as DORF. The fact that the battery covers, for instance, had the Ford oval moulded into them should have made nonsense of the deception, but the customs officers never seemed to notice.

At each Arab border we had to declare the make of our trucks, among a slew of information that each customs post required. It often made us smile to hear a driver solemnly declare that he was driving a Dorf, or a Cummins, but on one occasion, entering Iraq, a young Norwegian driver declared his truck as a Ford. There was an audible gasp from the rest of us, but the customs officer didn't notice, or maybe he didn't care.

It's a measure of how well suited to long-distance work the Transconti was, that operators would take the risk of extra hassle when sending the truck to the Middle East, when there were so many alternative trucks from which to choose. But there was no doubt that its durable and reliable driveline, and spacious, high-mounted cab, made it an ideal truck for long-haul routes, where these virtues outweigh the importance of a light tare weight.

It's clear from the many people Patrick quotes in this book that the Transconti didn't deserve such a short life, at least as far as it appealed to drivers and operators alike. However, Patrick also points to the main reason for its demise: it didn't make enough money for its maker. At the Transcontinental's launch, a journalist asked a senior Ford executive what part of the truck Ford actually made, and was told, 'the profit'. If only that had been true.

GEORGE BENNETT

The Blue Oval and Commercial Vehicles

Henry Ford, without doubt, did more to bring motoring to the masses than any other pioneering motor manufacturer of the early twentieth century. Simple, robust and soundly engineered, Ford cars were also affordable thanks to parts sharing and streamlined mass-production techniques. Even those who are not fans of the Blue Oval should be thankful that Henry pursued his dreams of motorcar manufacture over a more certain life on the family farm, for his success in this field changed, by necessity to compete, the products and practices of all motor manufacturers for the better.

The Ford Motor Company was officially registered in 1903, following two previous ventures – the second of which resulted in the formation of Cadillac – and production started with the Model A. More models followed in the next year and by 1906 nearly 15,000 cars had been produced. As far as commercial vehicles are concerned, we must move on to 1908 and the introduction of the ubiquitous Model T, or 'Tin Lizzie' as it was to become affectionately known. This simple car chassis ended up being perfectly easy to adapt into a useable commercial vehicle; engineers soon found that any number of body types, from basic flatbed to specialised custom body could easily be mounted. Utilised by anyone

At the time of writing in 2010, Transit production stood at over six million examples since it was introduced in 1965. The ultra-versatile van has been adapted for use in all manner of ways over the years. From ice cream van to mobile library and tipper truck to fire engine, its adaptability has been remarkable. Coupled to sound and reliable car-based mechanical components the Transit could hardly fail. Luton bodywork was extremely popular with furniture companies and did much to revolutionise the 'self move' market during the 1970s. This example has a lightweight aluminium body by Capital Coachworks of Norwood, South London. (Photo: Ian Walker, Ford Motor Company)

with a need to move goods, from farmers to government bodies, the T's success in this field, and as a motor car, prompted the introduction, in 1914, of Ford's famous production-line method devised to meet the incredible demand.

In 1911 Ford came to England and established manufacturing at Trafford Park, Manchester. The world's first mechanised war was not far away and the conflict of 1914–1918 saw truck-chassis production increase to incredible numbers, even by Ford standards. The subsequent glut of vehicles, available relatively cheaply following hostilities, did much to further powered transport in the civilian sector and saw more and more businesses able to convert from the traditional horse and cart to the internal-combustion-engine truck. With military-trained drivers and mechanics in abundance and a new understanding of powered logistics developed during the war, the modern transport system, as we know it, began to take shape.

The Model T's success as a light truck prompted the introduction of a purpose-built commercial vehicle in 1918, the TT 1-Ton chassis. The TT was largely the same as the motor car chassis, but utilised a slightly modified version of the same four-cylinder engine with the epicyclic gearbox and an overhead worm drive axle. Springs on the rear were of higher capacity and the rear wheels were shod

The D-series range covered the 6- to 28-tonne categories and endeared itself to thrifty operators, truly little trucks with big hearts. This smart example was one of 12 such vehicles supplied to Pricerite by Haynes and marked the first commercial-vehicle sale for young salesmen Ian Walker, who went on to become Sales Director for trucks. The 16-ton D1616 chassis were extended by Baico to give a wheelbase of 22 feet 7 inches before Freight Bonallack installed the 28 feet 10 inches aluminium alloy van bodies. Although not actively chilled, the trucks were heavily insulated with expanded polyurethane slabs to protect the fresh produce loads, which were delivered from a packing plant in Swanley, Kent to the company's supermarkets throughout the southeast. (Photo: Ian Walker; Ford Motor Company)

As a precursor to the heavy truck project, Ford did assemble three experimental D-series trucks on 6x4 chassis featuring a unique double-engine installation. The twin Dorset engines gave a combined 240 bhp, enough for a heavy truck at the time, and drove an axle each. The prototypes featured a slightly raised version of the standard D1000 cab, which could never have been taken seriously for long-distance work and with issues over weight, technical complexity and reliability, it is doubtful if the project was ever really intended for production. More likely, it was a shop window for Ford's engineering capabilities which also served as a particularly juicy red herring to fellow Anglo-American rivals, Bedford, whose design team were also known to be working on a heavy truck project. However, three prototypes did complete evaluation trials with selected operators including, BRS and Hilton Transport Services. (Photo: Ford Motor Company)

with solid tyres, though this was later changed to pneumatic type. A useful eight-foot load platform ran back from the engine bulkhead. This also had to accommodate the driver's cab, but nevertheless, with a vehicle track just 3.5 inches shy of five feet, it still offered a generous load area. The British government had been importing the TT chassis for some time, putting examples to use throughout the world in areas of national interest, so it was already well proven when it became generally available to the public in mid-1919. Trafford Park took up production of rolling chassis and later also offered complete trucks fitted with bodywork.

In 1925, Ford identified Dagenham as a prime site for development. This would help to relieve the Manchester plant, which could be extended no more and was now working to its maximum capacity, and provide the company with an ideal location from which to export orders to Europe and beyond. Ford of Britain was established in 1928 and work on the Dagenham site commenced in 1929. Although the Transcontinental was still some 66 years away at this point, these events are still very significant to the story as it was at this time

that Ford of Britain gained its own identity and ideas. From this point on, the products became distinctly tailored to the home market and more suited to the operating requirements and conditions of the UK, which were very different to those of the USA. Collaborations with established British firms, such as Hampshire-based County Commercial Cars, an enduring relationship covering multi-drive conversion of Ford products, began to bear fruit. From 1933, Ford of Britain trucks were marketed under the Fordson name and this remained the case until 1939 when it was changed to Fordson Thames.

Once again, war requirements fuelled production from 1939 to 1945 and, once again, war surplus vehicles flooded the market following the end of hostilities. Britain, although victorious, emerged battered and bruised, along with the rest of Europe, in a desperate state with an urgent need to rebuild and modernise. At this point, Ford of Britain started to develop the laddered commercial vehicle system, which, in principle, is still with us today. In this system, car-derived vans give way to purpose-designed vans, then light trucks, then medium trucks and finally, though not in Ford of Britain's case until 1974, heavy trucks.

Concept, Elba & H-Series
Something's Brewing

The heavy truck project, which would ultimately become the Transcontinental, is generally regarded to have had its inception early in 1971. At that time, pre-oil crisis, Ford of Europe was riding the crest of a wave, enjoying buoyant sales throughout its entire range. Crucially for the heavy truck project, commercial-vehicle production was particularly strong with the Transit and D-series, which were introduced in 1965, selling in huge numbers. By 1972 the project was well under way and the development team, under the indomitable Charlie Baldwin, had been set a date less than 36 months away for the first production example to be rolled out. The new heavy truck was to have an operating goal of 42 tons, ruling out any further development of the D-series, which at its most powerful had hit the design buffers at 28 tons. Plans to adapt a European version of a truck from the US range, the successful W-series, were deemed unsuitable on cost grounds. However, the US Louisville, or L-series, was identified as a good base from which to start and several complete trucks were shipped over to Dunton where they were stripped back to the bare chassis as a starting point for the heavy truck concept vehicles.

The L-series chassis was notable for its immense strength – around twice that offered by European manufacturers at the time – and flexibility. The pressed side frames were only 7.9-mm thick, but as they were manufactured from high-tensile steel no additional flitching was required to bolster the bolt in cross members. The chassis in this form was adopted for the production trucks. With nothing useful in the corporate parts bin to assist in the building of a heavy truck, besides a front axle and hub assembly used for the heaviest D-series, Ford's designers were obliged to head down the route of proprietary components. This was, and is, common practice for US truck manufacturers, including Ford, and, indeed, certain British firms at the time too, but was something that the strong European competition, such as Volvo, Scania and to a slightly lesser extent, DAF and Mercedes, did not entertain. The big advantage of the proprietary route for Ford was the ready availability of tried and tested components without the prohibitive costs of design, tooling, manufacture and testing. Since two of the key aspects of the new truck were extended service intervals of 12,000 miles and extreme long life, only the very best and most reliable of components would be considered. So Ford's designers and engineers decided to utilise the 'holy trinity' of Cummins/Fuller/Rockwell for the driveline. This was a combination that had literally millions of miles behind it on US highways and was highly regarded by drivers, service personnel and accountants alike.

By 1973, ELBA prototypes, as the vehicles were known, with the Cummins/Fuller/Rockwell drivelines were amassing thousands of test miles throughout Europe. The ELBA codename was derived from Ex-Louisville Berliet Assembly and referred to the origin of two of the major components for the new truck, the chassis and cab. *(Photos: Patrick Dyer)*

Brand-new Berliet cabs, fully trimmed and complete, including badges, wait on delivery pallets at Ford's Truck Prototype Shop at Dunton, where the original concept trucks were put together. Each ELBA prototype chassis carried a code number that started XB16. This cab was destined for XB167, its number being marked on the windscreen. All the major components for each truck were marked in this way. Berliet's superb cab was constructed from 465 parts held together by 5,500 spot welds and over 2,500 metres of seam welds. Note the distinctive engine locomotive emblem, which Berliet adopted following a licensing deal with the American Locomotive Company in the early 1900s. *(Photo: Ford Motor Company)*

The frame and Cummins engine of XB166 await further components. The very first ELBA prototypes were assembled on US L-series (Louisville) chassis, which were shipped to the UK as complete trucks. Dunton engineers subsequently stripped these back to the bare frames, but the L-series ancestry was plain to see, especially in the height of the cross member behind the engine, which on the US truck roughly corresponded with the cab's forward bulkhead. Later chassis were imported as unassembled side frames and cross members. *(Photo: Ford Motor Company)*

Although bearing little relation to the Transcontinental's final production cab mount, this very early design still retained the principle of coil springs and shocks to provide the best possible ride; this at a time when most rivals, including Berliet, offered rubber blocks as cab suspension. Note the L-series diesel tank, which has been relocated to the right-hand chassis rail rendering its cut out step and foot tread on the top unusable. Also, the air tanks, which occupy the final Transcontinental locations, albeit much changed and refined for production, suggesting that the original remit from the designers and engineers was spot on. Also of interest on this example is the temporary sound insulation board that has been placed, rather crudely, between the engine and front wings.

(Photos: Ford Motor Company)

ELBA prototype XB163 was one of the earliest completed and from this angle looks similar to a contemporary Berliet, with the exception of the quadruple headlights mounted in recesses in the bumper. The bumper itself shows clear ancestry to the final production item of the Transcontinental with the distinctive raised centre section and four-bolt mounting on the front face. The cab corner panels, though similar to Berliet items, were without headlights and featured a different side-light/indicator assembly. Note the tiny driver's mirror and Berliet indicator assembly beside the door handle. The latter was removed from some prototypes and would eventually be located on the edge of the lower corner panel for production trucks. (Photo: Ford Motor Company)

The big doors of the Berliet cab allowed good access, despite the three-step climb, and the door aperture was flanked with stout grab handles to aid the ascent. Here, the lower plastic dress panel of the door is clearly seen below the metal carcass of the main assembly. The distinctive 'chocolate block' plastic trim was tough, hard-wearing and continued through the vertical face of the lower dash. It was also mirrored around the top of the cab for the shelf above the windscreen and trim panels over the doors and windows. Note the socket-type ventilator in the shelf panel, which controlled the flow of fresh air to the cab through the vents at the top of the windscreen. *(Photos: Ford Motor Company)*

Following the initial concept testing, which was carried out beyond the public's gaze at Ford's Boreham facility, engineers ramped up the programme and undertook extensive trials in more challenging climates, such as this cold weather testing, carried out in Finland. Note that XB164 has a full UK registration (actually an Essex OO number), and not trade plates. It also features a different design of bumper and grille compared to XB163, the former bearing some resemblance to that of the Seddon Atkinson 400 series, which would also arrive in 1975 a little behind the Transcontinental. While not as sophisticated in terms of cab suspension, Seddon's 400 was a worthy adversary for the Transcontinental and could be ordered with similar driveline specifications, including Cummins/Fuller combinations. *(Photo: Ford Motor Company)*

Dunton, though not the prototype shop, also provided the assembly area for the initial trial trucks destined for service with selected operators. This large, well-lit area provided the ideal location for small-scale production. Studies conducted on the construction of the trucks were invaluable in setting up the proper Transcontinental assembly line in the Amsterdam plant. Note the final version of the bumper which awaits fitment in the upper photograph – though the rather unfortunate-looking main grille is still of prototype design at this stage – and the large, aftercooled Cummins engine awaiting fitment in the background of the lower photograph.

(Photos: Ford Motor Company)

Thankfully, the various early designs of grille seen on the ELBA prototypes did not get approval for production. It was down to the designers at Aveley to come up with something special to dress the lower half of the cab and this, the 'cab cube', is what they came up with. It is hard to imagine now that anything better could ever have been designed for the Transcontinental. The new panels completely changed the appearance of the cab, giving it an even tougher look and stamping 'Ford' on it in no uncertain terms. Here the 'cab cube' panels, probably only modelled in clay or plaster at this stage, are married to the main cab for the first time. Note the Berliet GR260 model designation, which is still on the cab trim strip. Berliet's GR designation was used for a rigid truck, while tractors were badged as TR. (Photos: Ford Motor Company)

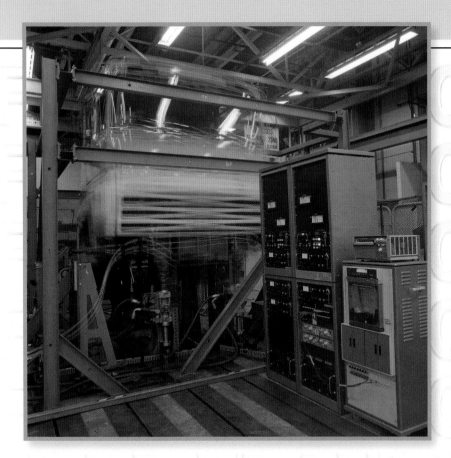

Obviously, Berliet had tested the KB2400 cab extensively before introducing it for its own use, a fact of which Ford would have been well aware. Ford was also no doubt privy to the details before making the decision to buy the Berliet cab, but with its own panels now wrapped around the lower section, re-testing was necessary and this hydraulic test rig was employed to speed up the process. The computer-controlled machine could simulate around 20 miles of rough going every minute, certainly enough to highlight any problems with the GFRP panels and/or the fixings. *(Photo: Ford Motor Company)*

A sight to make vehicle restorers weep! Brand-new KB2400 cabs, resplendent in fresh paint, trundle down the line at Ford's Amsterdam plant. Initially, Ford purchased complete cabs from Berliet, which were shipped by road, four cabs to a truck; this figure was drastically increased to 16 per truck once Ford started to take the cabs in kit form for assembly by the Amsterdam workforce. Note how modern and uncluttered the 1975 plant looks, even by today's standards. *(Photo: Ford Motor Company)*

A heart in mouth moment on the production line. The moment that a Transcontinental's cab and chassis came together was a delicate and tense operation for all concerned. Cabs were fully glazed, wired and largely trimmed out by this stage as such operations were much easier with the shell at ground level. The Ford dress panels, however, would be added later as part of the final fitting out; at this point, the elevated position on the chassis was an advantage. Note the extensive padding around the cab-lifting gantry. (Photo: Ford Motor Company)

At the time of its release, the Transcontinental offered one of the best interiors for drivers. The cabs were roomy, light and had excellent sound insulation. There were subtle differences to Berliet's own offering with Ford re-engineering the steering column to change the driving position and sourcing its own seating and bunks, though the option of a third seat was retained. The optional upper bunk stowed flat against the roof when not in use, leaving an un-obscured view through the rear windows. Ford also opted to delete the fake wood finish from the glove box lids and door cards, only retaining it for the main instrument panel. Note the optional third seat fitted to this example. *(Photo: Ford Motor Company)*

A small number of trusted hauliers were chosen for field trials of the H-series and Hays joined companies such as Silver Roadways and Bridon in its testing. The trial vehicles were few and far between and also a little camera shy; to spot one in the wild, so to speak, was a major coup and the author salutes the photographer for this sterling effort. Hays were no strangers to operating slightly unusual machinery. While not prototypes like the H-series, it did run a large number of rare, for the UK, Volvo G88 tractors on this work too. UMC 610M was later updated with the final production grille, but always retained the prototype front wings with the different profile. Most of the operators on the test programme chose to purchase the vehicles, no doubt at a very good price, after the trials. *(Photo: Adrian Cypher)*

Two versions of early H-series trucks seen abroad. Both of these examples have the final production grille and bumper but retain the earlier design of front wing, itself an evolution of previous ELBA designs, and door bottoms. Although close to the finished design that saw Transcontinental production, this version of front wing had a wider vertical face and less depth from the cab trim strip. The corresponding difference in the design of the lower door panel when compared to the production item was only noticeable in the shallower depth at the rear below the door handle. No production Transcontinentals were delivered like this, but the first Transcontinental brochures did feature them, even on the cover; indeed, the West-Friesland wagon and drag, devoid of company name, made just such an appearance. (Photos: Ford Motor Company)

Transcontinental Mk 1
Dizzy Heights

The towering Transcontinental, a full 3.24 metres tall, received its official launch at the Amsterdam plant, where it was to be assembled, on 30 April 1975. In a masterstroke of marketing, the H-series was renamed Transcontinental for its public debut; however, it was always to be known by both the new name and the designation of H-series. Indeed, model identification was HA for articulated units and H or HT for rigid trucks for the full nine years of production. Just prior to the official launch, the press were invited to meet and drive examples from the range at a test facility in the UK; there was also a hand-over of the first production example, a 4x2 unit bought by Simons International for operation on its Middle East routes.

For the production chassis Ford adopted the high-tensile, heat-treated side frames of the US L-series (Louisville), which were built up with bolt-in cross members, sourced from a company in Denmark, to form the traditional ladder-style item. All necessary holes, for mounting purposes etc, were drilled in the web of the side frames, leaving the top and bottom flanges clear to optimise strength and ease repair. All wiring and pipes were neatly routed in straight lines and were protected by the top flange. The whole assembly was acid-etched prior to painting with tough titanium-based paint. Initially, Ford offered two wheelbases for 4x2 units, one for 6x4 units, one for 4x2 rigids and one for 6x4 rigids.

Suspension, front and rear, was provided by low rate, semi-elliptical, multi-leaf springs with double-acting shock absorbers, which damped in both directions. The front springs were mounted on fixed pins at one end and shackles at the other, all with rubber bushes. The rear springs varied depending on the spec of the vehicle, but were attached in a similar fashion to those at the front, but with the rear shackle inverted. Both the front and rear arrangements were backed up by generous anti-roll bars to counter the kinetic effects of cornering. In the interest of reducing service time and effecting repairs at the roadside, the spring hangers featured a removable centre section, negating the need to burn out the old shackle pins when changing springs.

The front axle came from the heaviest of the D-series range and was an 'I' section steel forging offering a nominal capacity of 7,500 kg. Unusually, for a heavy truck, the lubrication of the hubs, front and rear, was via oil rather than the more usual grease. The reason for this was that oil offered immediate lubrication on moving off, with no reduced protection during a warm-up period, and thus far longer life from the components.

All rear axles were manufactured by Rockwell, with 4x2 vehicles being fitted with either the 10-tonne R170 or 11.5-tonne R180 item. Both units were fully floating single-reduction designs chosen for the minimal power drain they offered and their particular suitability for long-distance, high-speed operation. The single-reduction design was also expected to provide up to twice the mileage of the equivalent double-reduction, or hub

reduction, type, which fitted with Ford's 'long-life low-maintenance' ethos for the truck. Both units offered an air-operated differential lock – although only as an option on the R170 – and two final drive ratios of 3.7:1 or 4.11:1. The R180 could also be fitted with a deep 4.63:1 ratio for heavier work. The double-drive unit of the 6x4 was Rockwell's sturdy SSHD unit with a capacity of 20 tonnes. The fully floating, single-reduction axles were married to a four-spring, balance-beam design to form the rear bogie and could be fitted with either a 4.11:1 or 4.63:1 final drive ratio. The front and rear springs of the bogie were linked, via shackles, to a central suspension arm with a compensator rod, which transmitted the reaction force from the front axle to the rear. This ensured that when the front axle rose over an obstruction, the rear axle would be physically pushed down to maintain contact with the ground. The SSHD was provided with normal differential locks on both axles as well as an inter-axle lock.

With a design capacity of up to 44 tonnes, the Transcontinental needed a good braking system and an air-operated two-line design was developed with the help of technical input from Girling. The system was fully EEC compliant, to cover projected markets, and was easily adaptable to suit countries that used a three-line system, such as the UK and France. The wedge-actuated brakes featured a two-leading-shoe design that provided a prodigious contact surface of 2,790 sq cm per axle. Linings were incredibly hard and offered a potential life of 60,000 miles. In a rather unusual move, the brake chambers were mounted onto the rear of the drum and acted directly onto the wedge mechanism, rather than the more common axle-mounting and remote-lever arrangements of many competitors. For safety, the front and rear brakes were on different circuits with trailer braking being maintained in the event of a failure on either one. There was also an emergency brake, controlled by a dashboard-mounted lever which, using the parking-brake system, braked all axles and the trailer in the event of a total failure on the service brake circuits. During emergency brake application, the pressure to the rear axle was restricted to reduce the possibility of jack knifing. An exhaust brake was also available in the form of an air-operated gate valve mounted between the manifold, behind the turbocharger, and the silencer. The valve was operated by a foot button near the driver's seat base that could be easily depressed with the heel of the free accelerator foot. An inhibitor switch on the accelerator linkage prevented accidental operation of the exhaust brake, while power was applied, and consequential engine damage. The parking brake was 'spring' type with each axle equipped with two spring chambers that kept the brakes permanently applied until enough air pressure was available in the system to overcome the spring's pressure. The circuit was operated by a control lever, with locking collar, mounted in a recess below the gear stick. The system was charged by a single cylinder, cam-driven compressor which supplied two 25-litre reservoirs, one for front and one for rear brakes, mounted under the battery tray along with the system's 'wet tank'. There was also a trailer reservoir, usually to be found mounted on the rear cross member. Another unusual feature was the use of small-bore plastic pipes for the brake lines. These were manufactured from a tough thermoplastic and offered the twin benefits of increased durability over metal types and improved pedal response and feel. The system was completed with an alcohol injector system to prevent moisture freezing in the lines and causing failures. The aluminium-bodied injector unit and reservoir was mounted on the chassis by the air tanks and added alcohol before the air was stored for use.

In 1975 the Cummins engine range centred around the superb six-cylinder, 14-litre NTC series, which Ford utilised in the Transcontinental to offer three output levels of 273, 308 and 340 bhp via varying degrees and combinations of turbocharging and aftercooling, the latter being Cummins' preferred approach to intercooling. To satisfy those operators that were still wary of turbocharged engines and that maybe did not require 308 bhp plus, Ford also engineered the new truck to accept the Cummins Super 252. This normally aspirated six-cylinder unit had a higher capacity of 15.18 litres and provided a lusty 245 bhp and generous 700 lb-ft of torque – just enough to out-gun an F88, at least on paper. However, the Super 252 was only really engineered for 32-ton operation and was thus only made available for UK-spec trucks and, due to low uptake, was soon dropped from the range altogether. All engines featured wet liners and a four-valve-per-cylinder design: two for inlet and two for exhaust. The two middle engines, the 273 and 308 bhp NTCs, ran to a surprisingly low maximum speed of just 1,950 rpm, way below most of the competition in 1975, while the Super 252 and 340 bhp NTC ran at a still respectable, 2,100 rpm. This was obviously good for reliability, but even better was the fact that maximum torque occurred between 1,300 and 1,400 rpm in all cases. This meant 300,000 miles of service was easily possible before a major overhaul was required and the potential for good fuel economy, if the unnecessary higher revs were avoided, was achievable. All engines were fed by Cummins' PT (Pressure Time) fuel injection system, which supplied diesel from a constant low-pressure loop maintained by the compressor-driven fuel pump mounted on the left of the engine. Metering to the six injectors, three in each cylinder head, was governed by push rods running off the engine's camshaft and was highly accurate, further aiding economy and reducing emissions.

In addition to being turbocharged, the two most powerful engines were also aftercooled. Much like intercooling, first introduced on a European truck two years earlier by DAF for its 2800 DKS, aftercooling was used to lower the temperature of the air from the turbocharger, which reduced its density and thus increased the volumetric efficiency of the cylinder to give more power without increasing capacity. Cummins' approach was to utilise a neat two-piece aluminium housing mounted on the left of the engine parallel to the cylinder heads containing a copper-alloy heat exchanger, which utilised engine coolant to reduce the temperature of the intake air by as much as 35 degrees. The unit was fed air from the turbocharger, mounted in the exhaust on the other side of the engine, via a distinct, flat-section trunking that ran over the top of the middle cylinder head. The aftercooler housing also doubled as the engine intake manifold. As well as increasing

power, the reduced air temperature enhanced component life in the top of the engine.

The engine line up for the Mk 1 Transcontinental offered operators an excellent range of performance from tried and trusted units. Unfortunately the engines were not light, carrying a hefty weight penalty of around 1,300 kg, but, more significantly, fuel returns were considerably worse than most competitors.

To best harness the performance of the Cummins engines, Fuller constant-mesh gearboxes were chosen. These, combined with the engines and axles, extended the US driveline philosophy and were in stark contrast to the European move towards synchromesh units, as championed at the time by Scania and Volvo. Ford engineers wagered that the greater strength, reliability and component life offered by constant-mesh gearboxes would offset the higher degree of skill required by the driver to operate it.

Two units were available, the RTO9513 13-speed and the RT9509-C nine-speed unit. Both were twin countershaft designs featuring a basic transmission of four forward speeds plus a crawler gear and reverse. The nine-speed unit then utilised a range change to double the forward speeds to eight (four low range and four high range) while retaining the crawler gear, and offered high and low range on reverse too. The 13-speed unit did the same, but also incorporated an overdrive on the four high-range gears, effectively creating four more speeds. The range change and, in the case of RTO9513, the overdrive units were contained in a separate auxiliary gearbox, which was bolted onto the rear of the main unit. Both the range change and overdrive functions were air operated from the auxiliary air tank and selected via a three-position switch on the gear knob.

The primary design of the gear-change linkage suited a left-hand drive layout, with right-hand drive achieved via transfer linkages across the top of the foremost cylinder head of the engine. However, in left- or right-hand drive, the Transcontinental was universally commended by journalists for having the best Fuller installation available, a crown it would retain throughout its nine-year production life.

Twin plate clutches from Spicer were of rigid disc design and could be specified with ceramic facings for heavy and frequent stop/start work or organic for normal applications. Ford also developed and fitted a clutch brake, which, through complete depression of the clutch pedal, allowed very fast gear changes to be made when moving off on gradients.

The crowning glory, and the Transcontinental's most striking feature, was the superb, ultra-high-profile cab from the French manufacturer, Berliet, but, befitting its importance, this will be covered in depth in a separate chapter. (See page 60.)

Transcontinental production commenced at Ford's Amsterdam plant in 1975. The facility had been officially opened in 1933 and had undergone massive expansion of nearly 100,000 square metres – at huge cost – to fulfil its new task. However, truck production was not a new venture on the site with both D-series and N-series (the German-market version) having been produced there, the latter briefly overlapping with early Transcontinental production. The site was also the home of Ford's truck parts warehouse.

Ford unveiled the new Transcontinental range to the UK press on Monday, 27 April 1975 in an event held at the Military Vehicle Experimental Establishment, Chobham, Surrey. The event also boasted demonstrations and test drives of various types, including a double-bottom outfit. The first production Transcontinental was ceremonially handed over at the event to Brian Gates of Gates Ford, by Mr Terence Beckett, then MD of Ford, who was later knighted. (Photo: Gates Ford, Ford Motor Company)

Sir Terence Beckett's meteoric career with Ford started in 1950. Within five years he became the company's youngest-ever Divisional Manager, aged just 32. His division was responsible for the Cortina, Transit and D-series and therefore was arguably one of the most important. He became MD in 1974 and Chief Executive in 1976. Beckett was also a director of ICI and served on many bodies, such as the Milk Marketing Board. From 1980 to 1987, he was Director General of the Confederation of British Industry (CBI). *(Photo: Gates Ford, Ford Motor Company)*

Journalists witnessed many tests during the launch, including one where engineers deliberately burst one front tyre of an articulated combination at 40 mph; thus, they became familiar with the truck's selling points such as the generous 70-degree tilt of the big cab. It was probably no accident that the first customer Transcontinental went to Simon International, a well-known Middle East operator. In 1975, at the height of the 'gold run', Ford could not have asked for a better endorsement of its new product. *(Photo: Gates Ford, Ford Motor Company)*

Another Middle East operator that was quick to try the Transcontinental was Carmans Transport (Brit-European) of Stoke-on-Trent. Ford had deliberately designed the Transcontinental to have a long service interval of 12,000 miles, which was enough to allow for return trips to the Middle East. This was a strong selling point for Ford, but, unfortunately, one that might not have been fully understood by those on less rigorous work. With a typical trip to the Middle East bringing in around £3,500-plus, the durable Transcontinental, costing around £16,000, could potentially re-coup its costs over five trips – assuming that all went well, that is! (Photo: Ford Motor Company)

Even with three years of arduous Middle Eastern miles under its wheels at the time of this photograph, JVT 356N still looks in remarkably good condition. Despite a proven and robust driveline of the 'old school', the big Ford was, in many other ways, a very sophisticated truck for this type of work. For example, it had an elaborate four-point cab suspension system that was unrivalled until the introduction of Volvo's F10/12 in 1977. It was a credit to Ford's engineers that the system could withstand the hammering of the routes to and from the Middle East. Step-frame tilts were great for the high-cube nature of the groupage-type loads that were common on the 'gold run', but drivers dreaded the tendency of the small tyres to overheat and blow. (Photo: Adrian Cypher)

As the Mk 1 Transcontinentals were devoid of any model designation, it was impossible to tell which Cummins engine was beneath the big cab. Initially the options were: Super 252 (15.18-litre normally aspirated), NTC 335E (14-litre turbocharged), NTC 355E (14-litre turbocharged and aftercooled), NTC 355 (14-litre turbocharged and aftercooled). The Mk 1 featured an unusual double-pole electrical system that didn't earth through the chassis. The split 12/24-volt system should have offered less opportunity for shorting out and also meant that it matched military standards, suggesting that Ford had an eye to that market. The photographer would often spot this well-travelled and highly decorated example at the Leigh Delamere services, usually carrying containers. *(Photo: Adrian Cypher)*

Ford, with its all-conquering DFV V8 engine and various sponsorship deals, enjoyed a very high profile in F1 in the 1970s and this extended into the paddock with cars, vans and, following its introduction in 1975, the Transcontinental. Many teams and support companies, such as Goodyear, took on examples of the high-profile truck. Race transporters enjoy a somewhat charmed existence and make excellent second-hand purchases. For example, this LHD Transcontinental looks to be in very good condition after at least six years' work. Note the rubber bonnet straps that have been fitted to the main grille. *(Photo: David Wakefield)*

Following the Transcontinental's launch in May 1975, Ford set up a road show in conjunction with the main component suppliers – Cummins, Fuller and Rockwell – called 'Transcontinental Drive Around'. The tour visited 17 venues around the UK, ranging from service stations to hotels, through the months of June and July of that year. The tour offered potential customers the chance to look over the trucks in detail, discuss their requirements and take test drives.

Ravenfleet was the haulage arm of Connells Builders Merchants in Framlingham, Suffolk and ran a number of Mk 1 Transcontinentals. KBJ 4N was an early example supplied by nearby A G Potter. The Transcontinental did not suffer side window fouling to the extent that Berliet's own trucks did, possibly because it was mounted that much higher, so it was unusual to see corner spray deflectors fitted as seen here. Jewsons eventually bought out Connells. *(Photo: Ford Motor Company)*

The French had a large selection of domestic manufacturers to choose from when the Transcontinental was introduced, but Ford had already made inroads into the medium sector with the D-series, which must have helped with acceptance for the new big models. Even in 1975, French hauliers enjoyed a sensible weight limit of 38 tonnes for artics within a maximum 15-metre length. At that weight and with such a vast amount of country to be covered, even on domestic work, the Transcontinental was operating in its design element. Note the longer 3.5-metre wheelbase of this unit and the Trilex wheels fitted to the trailer. (Photo: Ford Motor Company)

The press and demo fleet were kept very busy in the months leading up to and after the Transcontinental's launch. Hauliers and the press were all keen to get their hands on these impressive new trucks and put them through their paces. Here, JEV 302N powers up the access ramp to a stretch of European motorway. This impressive 6x4 drawbar outfit had consecutively numbered stablemates including JEV 300N, an HA4231 4x2 unit, and JEV 403N, also an HA4231 4x2 unit, which were the first Transcontinentals to undergo full tests by Commercial Motor and Truck magazine respectively. There was also an H4227 4x2 drawbar, JEV 303N, and an HA4227 6x4 unit, JEV 301N. Note the Ford-jacketed crew aboard 302N.

(Photo: Gates Ford, Ford Motor Company)

As own-account operators go, it would be difficult to find one more specialised than the Welsh National Opera (WNO), with sets, costumes and an orchestra to transport around the UK and beyond. In 1975, the WNO bought its first two Transcontinentals, early Mk 1 types registered on P plates. The trucks were purchased as the company's touring pattern grew and replaced a much-unloved AEC Mercury, which had been supported by hired-in vehicles as and when required. The hiring of extra trucks continued, but the Transcontinentals took on the bulk of the work and performed the task so well that those involved still speak fondly of them to this day. Loads may not have been all that heavy, but the trucks were worked hard with schedules that were tight and inflexible. Here we see KBO 780P sporting its first style of livery when brand new in 1975 and, somewhat later, with the WNO's revised livery and logo plus a good layer of road grime to prove just how hard the trucks were worked.

(Photo: Ford Motor Company [main]; Mark & Kate Terrell [inset])

Here the WNO's two early units are seen parked up at the company's storage facility on the Penarth Industrial Estate outside Cardiff. This was a new development at the time, built on the site of the old docks, which has since been cleared and redeveloped into Penarth Marina. Opposite the WNO was R&D Transport, an old-style haulage firm that also ran a couple of Transcontinentals. Sometimes, when touring work was quiet, the WNO's trucks would subcontract to this company, mainly hauling loads of steel – a stark contrast to the usual work of the trucks but well within their capabilities. Note the absence of Ford lettering on the second example.
(Photo: Mark & Kate Terrell)

By the time of the 1975–1976 P registrations, Transcontinentals were becoming far more numerous; indeed, the 1,000th chassis rolled off the Dutch production line in May 1976 – one year after the launch. While oil and water levels could be checked physically via the front panel and grille, the Transcontinental also featured 'pre-flight' switches for these, along with electrical system checks, in the header rail above the driving position. With a cab height well over three metres, the Transcontinental towered over all European production trucks of its time. It is fitting that a company named Gulliver's Hire, which featured the giant of the story in its livery, operated examples of the big Ford.
(Photo: Adrian Cypher)

Ford was bullish in the promotion of the 6x4 Transcontinental and early examples were frequently loaned to the press and operators for evaluation. This was brave behaviour, considering the range was already viewed as being on the heavy side, even in a 4x2 configuration, but maybe confirms the theory that Ford really had anticipated a higher weight limit of at least 38 tonnes for the UK. This handsome example would have tipped the scales at around eight tons, hard to justify at the 32-ton limit, but, of course, there were many operators that could use this sort of unit, even in the UK, and the type was popular on the continent for general haulage at the higher weights available there. *(Photo: Adrian Cypher)*

Weymouth docks, a busy fusion of ships, trucks and cargo, and a fine study in the art of roping and sheeting provided by the driver of this smart Transcontinental. The 4x2 tractor was available in the UK with the wheelbase options of 3.07 metres (121 inches) or 3.5 metres (138 inches) – this example is the former of the two. The longer wheelbase extended the overall length of the chassis by 432 mm, while the rear overhang remained the same at 1,010 mm. Note the after-market upgrade to wider mirrors on this example. *(Photo: Adrian Cypher)*

As this recovery operator was not running on trade plates and the age of the adjacent Mercedes horse box is known, it is safe to say that this Transcontinental was still plying its trade after at least twelve years on the road. The sturdy Louisville frame and robust driveline of the Transcontinental were designed for long-life operation and extended service intervals. This may have made the Ford heavier and more expensive than some rivals, but total life costs would have been significantly better. Had more operators realised that, then Transcontinental sales could have rivalled those of the F88 and LB111. *(Photo: Adrian Cypher)*

Lou Thurgood bought LMD 645P, his first Transcontinental, in January 1978 from Prouts on the Old Kent Road. The truck was ex-Brain haulage; one of a batch of six disposed of from the huge Essex-based fleet and was first registered in April 1976. Lou paid £11,000, around £5,000 less than the truck would have cost new some 21 months earlier. The truck was finished in Ford Carnival Red, the colour Lou would adopt as the base for his livery from then on. Lou's young son Alan is literally learning the ropes on a substantial load of paper. *(Photo: Lou Thurgood)*

Headboard gone, air horns in place, a coat of paint for the bumper, his name on the door and 'Phantom 309' legend in place, Lou poses with his pride and joy. Lou was no stranger to Ford commercials as he'd owned three Thames Traders and a D-series prior to the Transcontinental. He had also tried early Scania LB110s and a couple of Guy Big Js with 180-bhp Gardner engines. During his long night trunks to and from Scotland, Lou would listen to the American Forces Network (AFN) and it was the Phantom 309 song that led to the naming of his truck. LMD 645P proved a reliable workhorse for Lou, the only problem area being the brakes. *(Photo: Lou Thurgood)*

Looking like a convoy? You'd be right. This fine line-up of Transcontinentals was just part of a 12-truck contingent assembled at Ford's Boreham facility early in 1976 for the filming of a Top of the Pops video to accompany the song 'Convoy' by C W McCall. The old airfield provided the perfect location, having been extensively used by Ford for the development of its potent rallying Escorts. Filming, carried out at night, was further hampered by fog and nearly ended in disaster after the barrier that the lead truck had to demolish at speed obscured its headlights. Also among the trucks was a Ford Louisville, possibly one of the original machines brought over for evaluation as the base for the first prototype Transcontinentals. The song was a great success for McCall, causing a boom in CB use and, of course, inspiring the film of the same name by Sam Peckinpah in 1978. *(Photo: Ford Motor Company)*

Transcontinental production hit the 1,500 mark after just seven months in December 1976, which created a wonderful public relations opportunity. Ford had orders for 400 Transcontinentals at the time of the launch, of which 50 per cent were destined for UK customers. They went so far as to estimate that production would be at 165 chassis a month by the year's end. When, in fact, production figures for 1975 (not a complete year) and 1976 are generally accepted to have been 934 and 1,751 respectively.

(Photo: Ford Motor Company)

Basking in strong sunlight, though nothing compared to what was waiting 6,000 miles away, MFA 413P loads at Carmans' depot. The company enjoyed good service from its earlier Transcontinental and purchased more vehicles in 1976. This was good news for Ford as Carmans were also big users of the Middle East stalwart, the F88; having the Transcontinental treated on equal footing with Volvo, an established market leader, was fantastic news for Ford. This wonderful example, with delightful matching tilt, is preparing for another epic trip at the company's Canal Road depot in Trowbridge. Note the optional air-conditioning that has been fitted to this unit. This feature is surely a must-have for any Middle East-bound vehicle, especially considering the large amount of glass in the Transcontinental cab. *(Photo: Adrian Cypher)*

Not looking quite as dapper as its departing stable mate, this returning unit and box van combination bears the grime of its journey. Berliet's superb KB2400 cab was slightly unusual in that it did not offer a roof hatch ventilator, when most of its rivals did, but instead provided fresh air ventilation through the two grilles at the top of the windscreen. There was a clearly defined, raised panel in the roof pressing, but neither Berliet nor Ford ever utilised it as a roof hatch. It was only later that Renault-branded cabs finally gained the feature much-loved by drivers. However, both Ford and Berliet used the panel pressing as the mounting point for an air-conditioning unit, which would be directly plumbed through to a neat control and dispensing housing below in the cab.

On the Ford, the pipes were neatly plumbed over the roof and down the centre line of the back panel. They were contained in a colour-matched conduit making them almost unnoticeable. The dedicated modification centre, close to the main plant at Amsterdam, was responsible for air-con installation, along with special paint finishes and tag axle conversions. *(Photo: Adrian Cypher)*

Gibraltar-based businessmen James Speed and Jerome Saccone merged their independent wine businesses in 1908. Strong links with the Royal Navy allowed the company to establish branches within the confines of RN bases throughout the world. This privileged position and unparalleled access allowed Saccone and Speed to prosper as the supplier of diplomatic booze to the embassies of Great Britain and many other countries. These two smart Transcontinentals were operated by the company's London branch in the mid-1970s. By then, the company was owned by Courage and provided the brewer with a ready-made wine and spirit division. A management buyout in the mid-1980s saw the company re-established back in its Gibraltar home. Note that the cab door trim strip on the nearest unit is actually the nearside item incorrectly fitted to the offside, resulting in the 'Transcontinental' script appearing further back than normal.

(Photo: Ford Motor Company)

Liquid loads like nothing better than a smooth ride for stability. The gearbox on the Transcontinental was generally regarded as the best Fuller installation in the business, offering fast, precise and smooth progress. All the more impressive, given that the main control arm always stayed on the left of the engine, was that although a further linkage was required for RHD vehicles, this had no adverse affects on the quality of the shift. Full credit for this must go to the Ford engineers that came up with the design.

Forth was owned by the Alexander family and operated from depots in Falkirk and Alloa, but was later absorbed into BRS. (Photo: Ford Motor Company)

In the early months of the Transcontinental, when Ford management were often out and about promoting the range, journalists frequently asked what Ford actually made. John MacLean, of Ford USA, simply replied, 'The profit', which, in actual fact, Ford didn't actually make either, at least not until the last machines were assembled at Sandbach by Foden.

The Transcontinental was very much constructed from proprietary components and, given that this was Ford Europe's first foray into heavy trucks, there was little for the company to draw on, even when taking into consideration the extensive car and medium truck parts available to the design engineers. However, Ford was responsible for producing the chassis frames and cross members, which were those used for the US-market Louisville range. Also, the front axle and hubs had D-series ancestry, Mk 1 Granada indicators were used in the bumper and an Escort light switch made it onto the dashboard.

(Photo: Ford Motor Company)

In another diversion from standard practice, early Transcontinentals were fitted with an additional steering ram acting on the opposite stub axle to the one controlled directly by the main, Burman, power-steering box. Ford claimed that this system, which worked at a lower hydraulic pressure, would be more reliable and fitted better with the long service interval design of the truck. Testers were divided in their response: some found it overly sensitive, while others praised its feel and precision.

(Photo: Ford Motor Company)

Sweden's weight limit and operating environment suited the big Ford nicely. However, the 42-tonne GCW of the Mk 1 Transcontinental fell a little short of the country's maximum 52-tonne limit for a 25-metre outfit running on six axles.

For Ford to chip into this market at all with such a new product was remarkable, especially given the extremely competent, globally dominant products on offer from the two domestic manufacturers. Note how disproportionate

the short wheelbase truck is in comparison to the trailer and the angled spare wheel rack, not of Ford origin, fitted behind the battery tray. (Photo: Ford Motor Company)

Early in 1977, Bram Smits Eurotransport of Antwerp took delivery of the 200th Transcontinental to be sold in Belgium; it was also the 2,500th Transcontinental to roll off the Amsterdam production line. Although this meant that at the time Ford was well on the way to its production target of 2,000 chassis a year; it actually fell short at 1,841. This time represented the peak of Transcontinental production.

Bram Smits' new unit was an HA4231 (308 bhp) with a 3.5-metre wheelbase and joined other identical units in the continental haulage fleet. *(Photo: Ford Motor Company)*

Ladbrokes obviously fancied the odds when taking on this Transcontinental, a highly unusual vehicle for betting company operations, but even more so as this was the prime mover of a drawbar outfit with matching trailer. What the vehicle's actual role encompassed is unclear; since Ladbrokes had nothing much to move besides betting slips. Possibly there was some amount of race track promotional activity involved and the high profile of the Transcontinental would have suited that well. The Lucky Seven bet was an accumulative-type bet based on the results of seven horses. *(Photo: Adrian Cypher)*

Pollock inherited JSR 102P when it took over the business of R S Pirnie of Pitlochry in 1977. The unit was less than two years old at the time and went on to perform well for Pollock. However, no further Transcontinental purchases were ever made, maybe the thirsty NTC engine could not match the miles per gallon figures of the rest of the fleet – mainly Scanias at the time – of Pollock's intensive trunking operations. The unit is pictured in the Mussleburgh yard, with fresh Pollock livery applied. Note the re-location of the Ford lettering to the main grille to free up space for the sign writing and the fleet name, Globetrotter, which pre-dated Volvo's use of that title by two years. (Photo: John W Henderson)

Ford offered three power take-off options for operators such as this, who required PTO-driven equipment to discharge loads or to power other machinery. All were Eaton-Fuller units and all mounted on the rear face of the transmission casing. If fitted, the air-actuated unit was engaged via a dash-mounted switch and could be operated with any of the first five low-range gears.

    The speed of the unit could also be governed by an optional hand idle control on the dashboard. The latter, if fitted, could be used to raise the engine idle speed when the engine was cold.

(Photo: Ford Motor Company)

A load of spare parts carried in a single-axle box van trailer more suited to a D-series and a four-car load rather uneconomically carried on a twin-axle low loader suggests Ford PR involvement in this photograph. However, the two Transcontinental units look suitably impressive even in these under-utilised roles. Ford did make good use of Transcontinentals within its own organisation, using them for parts movements between factories and other similar duties. This photograph was supposedly taken in 1979, but the two units seem to be pre-1978 Mk 1s in remarkably good condition. *(Photo: Ford Motor Company)*

As the door frames of the Berliet cab were so thin, the mirror brackets had to be mounted on the cab's A-pillar, in a similar fashion to the Leyland Marathon. Some drivers found pushing the passenger side bracket forward so that the mirror could be viewed through the windscreen gave a better view down the side of the vehicle. Despite the position of the mounting brackets, it was possible to retain the full 90-degree opening of the door if the mirrors were carefully positioned. The roof spoiler fitted to this tidy example suggests that plant and machinery movements were not necessarily the normal type of work undertaken; although the roof beacons would possibly contradict that theory. However, what is clear from this photograph, taken at Popham services on the M27, is that the Transcontinental was an adaptable design which, given that this unit was close to 20 years old at the time, was also capable of very long service indeed. *(Photo: Clive Davis)*

Ford's PR department saw an excellent opportunity for comparisons with this stunning photograph and used it to great effect in the 1977 Transcontinental brochure. Engineering excellence applied to both the suspension bridge and Ford's sophisticated four-point suspension cab. It must not be forgotten how advanced the Transcontinental's technology was when it was introduced in 1975. Volvo and Scania had both done a great deal to improve the driver's lot at the end of the previous decade, but were, respectively, two and six years behind Ford in offering four-point cab suspension systems. *(Photo: Ford Motor Company)*

The late Colin Mynard poses with NKM 11P, the first Transcontinental purchased by Birdale International Ltd for its service to and from the Middle East. The truck was supplied by Haynes of Maidstone and had the short, 121-inch wheelbase. The truck performed well, but Birdale's subsequent Transcontinental tractors were ordered with the longer wheelbase as the company favoured a five-foot kingpin position on its trailers to transfer more weight to the drive axle, which aided traction on inclines and in otherwise poor conditions.

As American foreign policy didn't win it many friends in the Middle East, Birdale found it prudent to list its Transcontinentals on Carnets de Passages as, 'Cummins Berliets' so as not to be directly associated with the American manufacturer. It also removed some badges, but did not find it necessary to remove the FORD lettering, as, unlike the blue oval, these were meaningless to the majority of customs officials.

Colin was one of Birdale's first drivers, joining the fledgling company in 1976 and staying for three years. *(Photo: Eric Wilson)*

Thanks to the introduction of the UK's new 38-tonne limit in May 1983, the slightly heavy Transcontinental became a viable proposition to many operators that had previously discounted it. This example, even as a 6x2 with tag axle, proved economic for TMC at the new weight. However, there would have been a useful saving in road tax for running on six axles rather than five, which may have helped this particular vehicle's case. It is a shame that Ford had already sealed the truck's fate by the time of the higher weight limit, as it would, no doubt, have found many new customers. Note the catwalk diesel tank and after-market wheel trims fitted to this example. *(Photo: David Wakefield)*

When OME 171R was first registered in 1977, along with OME 170R, it was a 4x2 chassis and was supplied to Kestral Transport by Gates Ford of Woodford. Kestral had big connections with Simon International, operators of the first customer Transcontinental on UK roads, and also operated out of Purfleet in Essex. The tag axle was probably added following the introduction of the new weight limit when after-market companies were doing a roaring trade in such conversions to 4x2 units.

(Photo: Gates Ford)

The Transcontinental, due to its towering height, could look a little narrow when photographed head on. However, it was actually 2.46 metres (98 inches) wide, typical for a premium tractor of the time, and a six-foot-plus driver would have no problem stretching out for the night on the bunk, even with the space allocated at one end for a wardrobe. The interior floor level, marked by the metal trim strip running around the cab, was a staggering 1.6 metres (64.5 inches) from the ground, but thanks to the three well-placed steps and stout grab handles either side of the door, entry and exit was generally recognised to be among the best in its class. Once in the pilot's seat, the driver was afforded a superb view of the road, even down and to the front thanks to the elevated seating and deep windscreen, while all-round glazing gave excellent views to the side and rear as well.

(Photo: Gates Ford)

Ian Walker of Haynes Ford hands over the keys of a very special truck to its new owner, Eric Wilson of Birdale International Ltd. Not only was TEV 767R Ford's ex-motor show truck, it was also one of the first, if not the very first, Transcontinental to be equipped with Ford's Long Haul Cab option pack. The base tractor unit in this case was an HA4231: HA for tractor, 42 for 42-tonne GCW and 31 indicating the output of the NTC 355E engine fitted to this particular vehicle. This engine was essentially the same as the top-power NTC 355 (340 bhp) being both turbocharged and aftercooled, but only ran to a maximum of 1,950 rpm, rather than 2,100, to give 308 bhp and a very useful 950 lb-ft of torque. The truck was Eric's seventh Transcontinental, joining four other tractor units and a pair of drawbars.

(Photo: Ian Walker, Kent Messenger)

Eric Wilson's Birdale International Ltd had a contract to deliver JCB products to Doha. Following a period of trialling on more 'local' trips to Germany, this load was to be the first of many runs to the Middle East for the smart white-and-orange-liveried truck. Unfortunately, and through no fault of Eric's, the truck was impounded in Saudi when its driver attempted to smuggle in 100 bottles of whisky and was never released from its desert compound. The 3.5-metre wheelbase allowed room for TEV 767R to be fitted with the largest capacity diesel tank of 600 litres. It also gave the necessary room for a York sliding fifth wheel. (Photo: Ian Walker, Kent Messenger)

Another early example displaying elements of the Long Haul Cab, this time a left-hand drive vehicle which is part of a Ford European show stand. While the headlight grilles are obvious, the double-skin roof and the storage cupboards which occupy the rear-window apertures – seen here through the tinted, laminated windscreen – are only barely visible. The tilted cab to the left shows the clever Berliet design that used a moulded ridge running around the front and side of the cab to direct rainwater towards the rear, preventing it from running off over the doors and dispensing with the need for a conventional gutter. Note that the big cab could only be tilted with the main grille in the open position.

(Photo: Berliet Foundation)

With no domestic manufacturer of its own, Denmark's transport system was dependant on imported machinery; this meant that all the major manufacturers were represented within the country's smartly prepared fleets. Ford enjoyed a good slice of the market, as did Leyland and Bedford, where the latter successfully marketed the TM. The TM was in many respects the Transcontinental's most direct rival, both being backed by a big US company and manufactured largely from proprietary components. The TM's biggest advantage over the Transcontinental was its comparatively light weight. Ultimately, however, the Transcontinental proved to be more durable, a fact which is supported by the higher numbers of machines that were still working long after the last TMs disappeared; Ministry of Defence vehicles being the exception.

(Photo: Ford Motor Company)

Long before the film of the same name, trucks from the huge Polar-Express fleet of Finland were a common sight on the TIR routes of Europe and beyond. This smart Transcontinental was making the long haul to the Middle East with this wide-axle spread trailer operating at Europe's common 38-tonne and 18-metre limit of the day. Domestic, Finnish law, however, allowed 20-metre artics at 42 tonnes, a weight that was far more appropriate for the big Ford: its original design weight being 42 tonnes. Finland's tough conditions, especially in the north of the country, called for tough trucks and, unsurprisingly, Volvo and Scania from neighbouring Sweden were common alongside the high-quality domestic products of Sisu. Despite this, Ford and other manufacturers did manage to make an impression on the market. (Photo: Ford Motor Company)

Various elements of the Transcontinental's design were aimed at stretching the service interval and the ultimate long life of components. The proven constant-mesh gearboxes from Fuller were a case in point: the rugged design being stronger than the synchromesh types offered by other manufacturers. Rather less obvious were items such the 'glicoated' driveshaft splines, which featured a special nylon coating that required no lubrication and reduced wear. The shafts themselves, manufactured by Spicer, were angled so as to reduce wear on the UV joints, especially when running at fast motorway speeds, which pointed to Ford's TIR aspirations of the truck. This smart example was operated out of Blandford, Dorset by the Panda soft drinks company. *(Photo: Ford Motor Company)*

Rather than follow the emerging trend among heavy vehicle manufacturers for snorkel-type air stacks running up the back of the cab, Ford opted for the traditional front-mounted item tucked behind the vehicle's bumper and attached to a bracket on the chassis. The large, two-stage filter chosen for the job was a Farr Unipamic item complete with separate moisture element. The housing was always mounted on the opposite side to the steering box. As such it would swap sides depending on a chassis being left- or right-hand drive configuration. The housing contained a sight gauge with a red warning indicator, which signalled the need to change the filter element. *(Photo: Marcus Lester)*

Even in the late 1970s, Spain's transport system was still geared towards rigid trucks with three- and four-axle twin steers predominant. However, for those leaving the country on TIR work, which suited the Transcontinental perfectly, the articulated truck/trailer was often employed at Spain's 16.5-metre and 38-tonne maximum. With many severe mountains, Spanish trucks were often fitted with a retarder, sometimes operating, rather unusually, on the trailer brakes. Ford offered a Telma Retarder as optional equipment on the Transcontinental. This device was mounted at the back of the transmission and used electro-magnets to slow the prop shaft. A four-position hand lever in the cab was used to select the amount of retardation required and a dash-mounted warning light illuminated during use. (Photo: Ford Motor Company)

The standard air tank layout on the Transcontinental was a three-reservoir system for the truck/tractor mounted under the battery tray with a fourth, for a trailer, mounted on one of the rear cross members. The tanks were of welded steel construction for durability. The front reservoir was the wet tank; the second was for the front circuit; and the third, the rear circuit. All three could be manually drained together as a pull-down cable connected the three valves. As an option, an automatic drain system could be specified, negating the need for the daily operation by the driver. The standard system also included an alcohol injector to prevent any moisture from freezing in the tanks and lines, the reservoir for this being chassis-mounted ahead of the wet tank. Many Transcontinentals, as here, were fitted with what appeared to be a fourth tank under the battery tray. In fact, this was a canister housing for an oil bypass filter. *(Photo: Marcus Lester)*

With Transcontinental production centred on the Amsterdam plant, it was little wonder that Dutch operators were keen to take on the Transcontinental as it was almost considered a domestic product. Established in the early 1930s, Ford's Dutch production facility was already huge, even before modification to accommodate Transcontinental production. Unfortunately, Ford's accounting process meant that when production of other vehicle ranges ceased at the plant, the Transcontinental became liable for the running costs of the entire site, including mothballed lines and other areas. The figures didn't stack up and as a result, the heavy truck range was, rather unfairly, never considered to be a profit maker during its time at Amsterdam. Note the neat spare wheel installation on this 3.5-metre wheelbase chassis and the steel half rear wings. *(Photo: Ford Motor Company)*

Although Switzerland had a domestic policy restricting trucks to a maximum width of just 2.3 metres, there was dispensation for operators working on international routes, which allowed operation of trucks, such as this fine Transcontinental drawbar outfit. Some manufacturers, such as Volvo, Scania and DAF offered specially adapted versions of their heavy trucks to satisfy the 2.3-metre limit. These would usually involve clever modification of a smaller cab from a lower range being grafted onto a top-weight chassis and/or the removal of any protruding peripheral items such as front wings. Thankfully, Ford never attempted a cut and shut D-series cabbed version of the Transcontinental to satisfy the Swiss market. *(Photo: Ford Motor Company)*

Ford went a long way to ensure the driver remained relaxed and comfortable. As well as particular attention to sound deadening and insulation, all major instruments, such as oil pressure and coolant temperature, read three o'clock when normal to prevent driver fatigue. This meant that a fleeting check was all that was required to monitor these functions. This well-preserved example photographed in the mid-1980s was clearly much cherished by its driver/owner.

(Photo: Marcus Lester)

This Austrian operator chose Ford over domestic manufacturers Saurer and Steyr for this pair of prime movers with drawbars. With severely mountainous terrain, including the Alps, big-power trucks were the order of the day for many Austrian operators, especially those with loads such as this; it is hard to imagine this pair being powered with anything less than the turbocharged and aftercooled NTC 355E offering 308 bhp. For starting the engine in cold weather, the Transcontinental was equipped with an ether injection system. This was controlled by the driver via a small control pump, which unscrewed for operation, at the base of the gear lever. The ether canister was mounted next to the inlet manifold and contained enough ether for around 130 cold starts. (Photo: Ford Motor Company)

This Italian drawbar milk tanker comprises some interesting axle combinations, especially on the trailer. The truck is fitted with a tag axle, which if an SVO item, was probably a York unit. Italian drivers often preferred to be on the right-hand side of the cab as it afforded a better view of the edge of the road in mountainous terrain. When moving off on a gradient, they would also have appreciated the Transcontinental's clutch brake, which allowed fast gear changes to be made without the need for double de-clutching. The brake was operated by pushing the pedal right to its stopping point, unlike normal operation with a double de-clutch method, which required only two-thirds depression of the pedal. The clutch brake was not recommended for general use as it prematurely wore the clutch plates. (Photo: Ford Motor Company)

Plain and simple presentation works well for this smart German Transcontinental. Germany, along with other countries with Ford production plants, seemed to warm to the Transcontinental, maybe in some way taking ownership of the trucks as a quasi-domestic product. Germany down-rated its controversial eight-bhp-per-tonne ruling in 1978 to just six bhp. However, this Mk 1 example would have needed to comply with the earlier ruling, meaning at least 304 bhp was required at 38 tonnes, a figure just covered by the penultimate NTC 355E and nicely exceeded by the top-of-the-range NTC 355, which had 340 bhp on tap. (Photo: Ford Motor Company)

Far from just jumping onto the Middle East bandwagon, Ford's offering, 'the Long Haul Cab', was logically thought out and superbly executed using high-quality components and fittings. The Long Haul Cab comprised four basic option packs, each of which contained a number of features, totalling 32 items in all. Key to driver comfort was the double-skin roof, which took the full force of the desert sun while providing a cool air cushion when on the move. The air conditioning was an equally important feature. Some features by necessity deleted others, such as the under-bunk storage area, which was only available if the lower bunk was removed. The bespoke refrigerator had a 22-litre capacity and was mounted neatly between the seats on two brackets with vibration insulators. Early refrigerators were simply on or off but later examples were fitted with a thermostatic control knob to allow a tailored temperature to be selected. The unit could run from the truck's batteries for 12 hours without the engine being started. As storage space was obviously an issue, Ford's designers also came up with brilliant unique items for the truck chassis, like the combined toolbox and water storage rack, seen here behind the battery box, which held 60 litres of water in three plastic jerry cans above a useful toolbox.

(Photo: Ford Motor Company (main); Ian Walker, Kent Messenger (inset))

By specifying window blanks for the side and rear windows, operators could gain more storage space for tinned food and similar items within the cab. Small cupboards were created in the rear panel by boxes that protruded out from the original window apertures. Also visible is the tidy installation of the air conditioning pipework, neatly covered by a conduit on the centre line of the rear panel. Security was a big issue for Middle East drivers and in this respect the Long Haul Cab could include locks for the cab-tilt mechanism and grilles and all fillers. It could also offer up to 10 padlocks, all operated by one common key, to secure other chassis-mounted items such as the battery cover, water carriers and wheel chocks. For the personal safety of the driver, extra interior door locks and an intruder alarm, which sounded the horn if the door was opened, could be specified. The two-ring cooker was fed from a gas bottle behind the passenger seat and came with splashguards, not in place here, for the sides. There was also a generous, centre-mounted table which, when in place, could be used from either seat.

(Photo: Ford Motor Company (main); Ian Walker, Kent Messenger (inset))

KB2400
The French Connection

Berliet's KB2400 cab caused a sensation when it was introduced on the company's GR and TR260 trucks in 1972. The KB2400, or 'Premiere' as it was known, was the first of the new generation of modern cab designs to emerge from the mainstream manufacturers in the 1970s and very much set the standard with a handsome, four-square design that optimised the space available within the legal exterior limits of the time.

The new cab had much to live up to as its predecessor, the 'Relaxe' cab of 1959, had itself done much to improve driver comfort and safety within an attractive design during the previous decade. The KB2400 did not disappoint.

The aptly named Premiere cab was an all-steel construction with two distinct halves separated by a waistline marked by a metal strip that ran around the sides and front. Above the waistline the cab was formed from spot and seam welded sheet metal panels and pressings, while below the metalwork was all bolted into position. The lower dress panels and front wings were all of GFRP (Glass Fibre Reinforced Plastic), which were attached to the lower section and brackets that hung below it. Being GFRP these panels gave Berliet, and later Ford, great scope to change and update the cab at a far more sustainable cost than would have been possible had re-tooling for metal panels been required.

The cab employed generous exterior dimensions and a near vertical windscreen to provide a roomy interior capable of containing three individual seats – a rather unusual feature for a premium truck – and two good-sized bunks. Combined with a large glass area of four square metres and a virtually flat floor, a light and airy environment for the driver and crew was created. The visibility afforded by the one-piece windscreen and large side and back windows was superb. Forward visibility was maintained, even in the worst conditions, by a three-wiper system, employing 460 mm blades, which swept 75 per cent of the 1.62 square metre screen. There was also an elaborate heating/demisting system with multiple vents along the base of the windscreen and side windows. The size of the windscreen dictated another unusual feature, roller blinds for sun visors. These ran on guides in the A-pillars and a central loop in the middle of the screen. Similar roller blinds could also be specified for the door windows as an option.

Much attention was placed on noise insulation, and Berliet made a point of mounting the cab high on the chassis, negating the need for an engine tunnel and allowing for an almost flat floor. The design meant lower noise levels were transmitted into the crew compartment from the mechanical components and also afforded the occupants across-the-cab access and easy entry to the bunks. The floor was completely watertight with all through holes for cables and linkages using specially designed seals, that of the gear stick

being an elaborate double-walled bellows, which actually formed an air cushion when the cab was lowered. A thick insulation material of double-skinned rubber mats with foam filling covered the entire floor. Even the door seals were specifically designed to reduce noise levels with lip seals on the outside edge and tubular joint seals on the inner, such was the importance placed on the comfort and well-being of the crew.

Cab suspension, although rudimentary compared to the later Transcontinental, was provided by three rubber blocks at the front and two at the rear, plus a suspension seat for the driver. While not revolutionary, the system worked well and was at least as good as anything else available at that time. The KB2400 was the first tilting cab produced by Berliet and it had a generous tilt angle of 70 degrees, enough to allow engine removal from above. A single double-acting hydraulic ram, powered by a manual pump mounted on the chassis side frame, controlled the tilting process and could hold the cab at any angle between zero and 70 degrees with the pump set in the intermediate position. The ram featured special nozzles in the cylinder to maintain the speed of descent should a feed line rupture during lowering and, being double-acting, also held the cab down when the pump was in the reverse state. However, there was also a robust automatic centre lock, which engaged as the cab settled onto its rear mounting. To aid service and repair an engine start switch was provided inside the chassis frame for use when the cab was tilted. For security the auxiliary starter could not be operated when the cab was in the lowered position.

Instruments which comprehensively covered the main functions of the truck were neatly laid out in a gently angled dashboard, designed to eliminate glare. There was also a central warning light that illuminated to highlight any defect that could affect the progress of the truck. The large 550 mm diameter steering wheel was a padded two-spoke design that allowed a clear view of the instruments at all times. The controls for the powerful heater/ventilation system were mounted in the vertical face of the dashboard. Driver and passenger enjoyed separate zones with two outlets each; the system could also aerate, completely changing the cab air in 45 seconds. Face level ventilation was provided by outlets in the shelf above the windscreen, which were fed directly from the distinct vents on the outside in the top panel above the screen. These could be fitted with additional blowers to allow operation when stationary.

The sleeper could be fitted with one or two bunks; if two bunks were fitted, then the upper one could be stowed flat against the ceiling when not in use and lowered onto support bars, which ran across the window, when required. Each bunk was equipped with a light and afforded each occupant 550 mm of headroom. The walls of the sleeper were lined with insulated foam panels with a breathable, perforated fabric covering. Curtains were provided for all rear windows and the berths could be isolated from the driving compartment by curtains behind the seats. There was also provision for an optional wardrobe at one end of the bunks.

The KB2400 remained unchanged until 1977 when Berliet raised the floor level in order to accommodate its new MDR 635 engine. Ford refused to take the new design and continued with the original pressings, subject to a 28 franc supplement per cab to cover Berliet's cost of producing both types alongside each other.

In the autumn of 1978, Berliet commissioned a one-off show truck featuring a raised roof. The GFRP roof was added by an independent body builder and the interior was fitted out with everything that a long-haul driver might need, including a chemical toilet and ubiquitous kitchen sink. No doubt Berliet were following the trend for Middle East cabs and surely took inspiration from Ford's own conversion on the Transcontinental, which appeared in 1976, especially with regard to the cupboards installed in the window apertures. Berliet's truck drew much attention and eventually became an option, known as 'The Centaure', with RHD versions becoming available in the early 1980s.

Since 1974, Berliet had effectively been part of Saviem, a conglomerate of French truck and bus manufacturers – including Renault – that were merged under a government directive. The deal was aimed at protecting France's domestic manufacturers, keeping them competitive in export markets that were key to their existence, and came with a generous 500 million francs of taxpayers' money as a sweetener. In 1978 the group became RVI (Renault Vehicle Industries) and in 1979, at the Frankfurt show, it was announced that all trucks would be branded as Renault from then on. This marked the disappearance of the Berliet name from the top weight TR trucks and Saviem from the mid and lightweights. However, the KB2400 would continue to provide Renault with its top-weight cab until 1996, a staggering 24 years after it was introduced. Along the way it received minor styling changes, courtesy of those cheap to change GFRP mouldings, and was twice remarketed, first as the R-series and later as the Major range. Inside, the cab received an improved dashboard with the introduction of the R310 and ever more luxurious and cosy fittings, further endearing it to long-haul drivers. From the mid-1980s, the high-roof version, now more modestly equipped and known as the 'Turboleader', became very popular and almost a standard fitment. Renault also developed an elaborate aerodynamic package consisting of a massive one-piece roof deflector, cab side extensions and under-bumper spoiler. Ford could have enjoyed a steady cab supply for a further 13 years had it decided to continue with Transcontinental production after 1983, and could have updated it as Renault did along the way to keep it fresh – a tantalising thought!

Ford's adoption of the KB2400 brought useful extra volume to Berliet's cab production line and the partnership shared the cost of developing the right-hand drive version, too. In addition to Ford, Berliet also supplied SONACOME (Société Nationale de Construction Mecanique) in Algeria with the KB2400. This was a joint venture overseen by the Algerian

Probably the smartest Berliet operated in the UK was that of Edwin Shirley Trucking. The Berliet joined the EST fleet when the company started to look at other makes of truck besides Volvo in the late 1970s. This dramatic image was originally destined for one of the company's infamous calendars, hence the hired trailer and one of the company founders, Roy Lamb, at the wheel. In the event the photograph was never used, but instead appeared as a centre spread in the June 1980 edition of Truck *magazine. EST's example was an early facelift model with revised grille and lights – styling changes that were similar to those made by Ford for its version – as well as Renault badging. The unit worked into the mid-1980s and was the regular truck for EST driver Iain Purdie. However, unlike DAF, which was also trialled by EST around the same time, the Renault did not spawn further purchases from the French manufacturer. (Photo: Edwin Shirley Trucking)*

Government, which produced Deutz-powered Berliet trucks and buses for the local market. To manage the cost of shipping to Algeria, SONACOME cabs were sent as CKD (Completely Knocked Down) kits, which Ford also swapped to after an initial period of receiving built-up cabs.

The smart drawbar combination run by M J Morris and Sons was unusual for UK operation and caught the attention of Ford's publicity department, which leaped at the opportunity to photograph the vehicle for brochures and literature. The flexibility that the drawbar combination afforded this owner offset any concerns over unladen weight and the curtainside access – at a time when that system was still in its infancy – proved an advantage during the loading and unloading process. Note the large-capacity diesel tank.

(Photo: Ford Motor Company)

With the battery cover removed it is possible to see the slightly unusual layout used for the Transcontinental's electrical storage. Instead of the more common method of using two 12-volt batteries to deliver the truck's 24-volt supply, Ford opted to use four six-volt batteries to achieve the same result. These were mounted next to each other in the generous battery tray and were retained by the shaped floor and a bolt-in bracket. In the interest of longevity, early Mk 1 Transcontinentals used 12 volts for certain parts of the electrical system such as the headlights and radio. Next to the batteries, and also protected by the cover when in place, was a useful toolbox on the front of which, when fitted, was the optional external ignition switch. This tidy example seems to be making full use of its TIR credentials, proudly displaying numerous destination stickers and flags.

(Photo: Adrian Cypher)

This Italian operator favoured right-hand drive for this exceptionally smart Transcontinental which it operated on international work from the port at Genoa. The Transcontinental's distinct, four-headlight system was controlled by a small lever mounted on the left of the steering column. This lever had two main positions: first, side and tail lights and second, the main headlamps. The main beam, which brought in the two inboard lamps, was controlled by the windscreen wiper function lever, which was also mounted on the left of the steering column. *(Photo: Ford Motor Company)*

In addition to the 107 UK dealers that Ford initially appointed to sell and service the Transcontinental, a huge £7 million investment was made to give coverage on the continent too. This gave the Transcontinental a great advantage over other home-grown products, some with similar Cummins/Fuller combinations, when being considered for continental work. No doubt the driver of this well-travelled, late model Mk 1 derived peace of mind from the back-up situation while on TIR routes throughout Europe and beyond.

(Photo: Willy Vos courtesy of Adrian Cypher)

This photograph must have been a PR coup for Ford back in 1978, and now, over 30 years later, it gives a great comparison of the different approach to truck design offered by two of the biggest producers of commercial vehicles at that time. When developing the SK range, Mercedes-Benz was very concerned with lowering the visual impact of the heavy truck. Much public consultation and testing resulted in the low, compact and soft-edged design, which became so familiar. In comparison the Transcontinental was a towering brute. Although Ford did not design the basic cab, the raised mounting and the revisions it made to the lower panels and bumper gave it a much tougher appearance than its Berliet/Renault cousins. Note how much taller the Transcontinental is, even with the Mercedes raised on the former's twin-boom lifting gear.

(Photo: Ford Motor Company)

The introduction of Roll on, Roll off (Ro-Ro) services to Malta in the late 1970s opened the door for companies such as Emmanuel Vella & Sons, which started its Express Trailers operation in response. This superb Mk 1 Transcontinental was probably exported from the UK after its original working life came to an end, but was a frequent return visitor, often spotted on the M4, complete with Maltese plates, servicing one of the company's overland contracts. Note the chassis locker mounted behind the diesel tank. (Photo: Adrian Cypher)

These two Transcontinentals owned by Welsh haulier Hicks International make a handsome pair resting in a UK service area. Due to political situations, Ford products were not always welcome in certain areas of the Middle East and it was not uncommon for Transcontinental drivers to change the order of the FORD lettering on the front of their trucks to deceive officials and locals. At least one driver, when alerted to a changed political position awaiting him at his final destination, purchased Berliet badges en route to shroud his truck's identity. Hicks' Transcontinentals were devoid of the lettering, whether this was to allow more room for the livery/sign writing or to avoid political problems abroad it certainly made for smart-looking trucks. Aside from Middle East work, Hicks was also a major distributor of tomatoes in the UK, which were imported through Cardiff. (Photo: Adrian Cypher)

The air bag was a major advancement in the field of recovery work and offered the prospect of righting vehicles in a safe and controlled manner, often with no further damage occurring during the process. The forward-thinking operator of this smart 6x4 Transcontinental, which keenly displays the availability of air bags, was obviously at the cutting edge of such technology back in 1978 and no doubt appreciated the forward thinking involved in the design of the truck too. The robust, four-spring balance beam 6x4 bogie featured Rockwell axles with cross-axle diff locks and an inter-axle lock between the two. Tractor units were fitted with an anti-roll bar on the rear axle only, while rigids also had one on the forward axle.

(Photo: Ford Motor Company)

This well-worked Transcontinental of Bodmin Transport seems to be sporting a replacement bumper, possibly of steel construction, judging by its sharp-edged finish. Despite its butch appearance the original GFRP (Glass Fibre Reinforced Plastic) bumper, though backed with steel, was always easily damaged. Note the relocated FORD lettering and GLC exemption plate, which suggests this unit was probably on fruit and vegetable work for the London markets.

(Photo: Marcus Lester)

The Transcontinental was fitted with a twin-wedge braking system, which offered a large braking surface on each axle via its two-leading-shoe design. With front axles designed to take around six tons of imposed loading, the front brakes were required to take on a high ratio of braking effort, too. Some UK operators did experience problems with the Transcontinental's brakes, often struggling to make the required performance on annual test. The accepted theory for these problems was that the Transcontinental always worked well below its optimum design weight, especially in the UK at 32 tons, and the subsequent glazing of the under-worked brake linings adversely affected performance. As if to prove the theory, double-bottom outfits operated by UK firms in the Middle and Far East at weights approaching 60 tons encountered no such problems.

(Photo: Marcus Lester)

FORD TRANSCONTINENTAL

With strong mechanical drivelines and an inherent durability, the role of the wrecker was often filled by elderly Transcontinental tractor units as evidenced by this pair – which were employed by Poole and Exeter Ford dealerships – following the transition to Iveco Ford Truck. Many Ford people were unimpressed by the merger which saw the heavy truck side of the business centred on Fiat-based machinery. At least one dealer persisted in replacing the small blue oval badges fitted to these vehicles with the bigger item of the Transcontinental and many, no doubt, derived a certain sense of pleasure in recovering the Fiat-based trucks with Transcontinentals like these, which were over 25 years old.

(Photos: Clive Davis)

This very capable looking machine advertised the service of vehicle recovery from both mainland continental Europe and the Middle East, which could have involved dragging a fully freighted truck and trailer many thousands of miles before repatriation, and, in the case of the latter, through some appalling conditions as well. Such an operation would have cost a pretty penny, but the alternative of leaving a vehicle to be picked clean of its useful parts was even more costly and inconvenient. This Liverpool-based 6x4 truck was equipped for most eventualities; its long wheelbase was packed with equipment and even accommodated a small workshop built behind the cab. (Photo: Ford Motor Company)

Safely back on home soil, this Transcontinental, owned by London-based Strada, looks imposing as the driver guns it out of Dover. RKC 911T, a late registered Mk 1, is fitted with the standard, 300-litre (65-gallon) diesel tank which in this case has been augmented with an after-market catwalk tank for extra capacity. Ford did offer a 460-litre (100-gallon) tank as an option. If fitted into the short wheelbase chassis the longer tank would virtually fill the available space between the front drop wings and the rear axle and incorporated a cut-away rear corner to clear the spring hanger. Note the interesting bumper modifications that have taken place here. (Photo: David Wakefield)

Transcontinental Mk 2
Weight Down, Power Up

Ford never rested on its laurels with the Transcontinental, or any other vehicle in its portfolio for that matter, with constant development and improvement always ongoing. Some refinements were not necessarily evident to the buyer, such as changes to production methods and component manufacturers, but the benefits that these changes brought to service life and operating costs were very real for the end users.

Since its introduction in Mk 1 guise, the Transcontinental had suffered from two major drawbacks. Firstly, it had been robustly designed for long life while operating at 42 tonnes and was consequently seen as heavy in some markets – particularly in the UK where such high gross weights were not permitted. Secondly, the superbly reliable and powerful Cummins NTC engines were thirsty, typically delivering mpg figures that were 10-15 per cent behind the competition. Some operators, those that worked on whole-life costs, understood that the weight and fuel figures were only part of the overall picture and that these were offset by the extended service intervals, reduced journey times and superb reliability that the Transcontinental delivered. However, Ford did have to address the problems, if only to appease the journalists and get a fair critique, so it launched the Mk 2 version at the Paris Salon in the autumn of 1978.

Useful weight savings were made for the Mk 2, mostly through changes in the suspension and steering. The front anti-roll bar was deleted from all but the lightest of the rigid chassis, the H3424, while the rear item was of a reduced diameter (36 mm) on all models. The length of the rear springs was reduced by 240 mm and the steering, now by Cam Gears and Plessey, reverted to a normal layout without the assisting ram that had been fitted to the Mk 1. Many other components, such as the air cleaner and starter motor, were replaced by lighter designs too. The changes, while not affecting performance, were enough to bring the weight of the Transcontinental in line with the majority of the competition. This was particularly true when viewed against strong European products with a continental spec, which meant tractor weights of around 7–7.3 tons depending on equipment.

Undoubtedly, the biggest news for the Mk 2 was the adoption of Cummins' new NTE engines across the entire Transcontinental range. Cummins' engineers in Europe and the USA had worked long and hard developing its new Formula-E series, the legendary 'big cams', to produce one of the most advanced and fuel-efficient engine ranges available at the time. Based on the previous 14-litre, six-cylinder design, the NTE range featured a modified block, to accept the larger camshaft, and was visually identifiable from the old NTC range by the more pronounced cam-follower housings. The block also featured revised stiffening ribs to reduce noise and vibration. The new camshaft was increased in diameter by 12 mm to 63 mm. As the Cummins' injection method was uniquely controlled by push-rods and rockers that were actuated from the camshaft, a higher injection pressure of 14,000 psi was possible, which was up to 15 per cent higher than the old NTC engines. As well as increased pressure, the fuel injection period was reduced to provide a cleaner, more efficient and controlled combustion that now occurred as close as possible to the theoretical ideal with the piston at top dead centre. Although dramatically increased at the injectors, the fuel pressure in the feed lines was maintained at the much lower rate of the lift-pump to minimalise the potential for leaks. To maximise the advantage of the changes in injection, a new piston crown featuring built-up edges around the valve pockets was employed and the compression ratio was raised to 15.3:1.

A new 'branched' exhaust manifold, tuned to maximise the pulse energy of the expelled gases, was developed especially to suit the characteristics of the new Holset HC3 turbocharger. Holset, of Huddersfield, had been absorbed into the Cummins group in 1975 and the HC3 was the first of the company's UK designed and manufactured units to be fitted to a production Cummins engine. Smaller and lighter than the previous unit, the HC3 featured a divided turbine design, with each rotor housed separately, and through efficient operation helped to provide near perfect fuel–air ratios to be delivered to the pistons over a wide speed and load range. This gave the NTE engines great flexibility and a low lugging nature that increased economy.

A revised water pump, with a smaller moulded impeller made of a non-metallic, phenolic material was fitted, which was more efficient and saved around 6.5 bhp. Further power losses were eliminated by reduced oil pump demand, thanks to a new oil thermostat that maintained an even temperature in the system, while improved lubrication of the con-rods was achieved by moving the oil passage holes. The big-end bearing shells now had thicker steel backs.

The two more powerful engines, the E350 and E370 were again aftercooled in the same manner as the old NTC range, with a heat exchanger unit that doubled as the intake manifold, but featured a lower compression ratio to the E290 of 14.3:1. This maintained reliability and was achieved by the use of a deeper piston bowl. The injection timing was slightly different too and the injectors featured nine holes rather than eight.

Engine speeds were down on the old NTCs, with the E290 and E350 running to a maximum of just 1,900 rpm and the big E370 running to 2,100 rpm. The two lower-powered units provided optimum performance and economy between 1,200 and 1,700 rpm, making them extremely flexible, which meant fewer gear changes. As well as the improved economy and increased power, the NTE engines were lighter than the old NTCs, the E290 being 36 kg lighter than its predecessor. This was a useful feature for all the truck manufacturers that used them but especially for Ford.

Ford, although slower to adopt the range than its rivals, announced the NTE-powered Transcontinental from October 1978 with the E290 rated at 240 and 270 bhp, the E350 at 315 bhp and the E370 at 345 bhp. All engines were now finished in light blue.

For the Mk 2, a conventional, chassis return electrical system became standard, though the double pole (insulated return) system was still available for those applications that required it. This marked a great improvement and reduced the risk of electrical fires caused by unskilled installations of additional electrical equipment. The four-battery layout of the Mk 1 was retained, but gone were the 12-volt headlights, the whole system now running on 24 volts. The handy circuit breaker system of the Mk 1 was retained. Conveniently located below the dashboard on the driver's side, the system comprised five reset buttons, each controlling four circuits.

Although unchanged, the chassis was now acid-primed prior to painting with a high-grade paint to give better adhesion of the coating and a more durable finish. Timely cosmetic changes to the Berliet cab resulted in an even better looking truck than the Mk 1. Gone were the FORD letters from the front panel, replaced by a modest 'blue oval' badge in the centre of the – now matt black – main grille. This followed the trend of Ford's entire line-up and gave the Transcontinental the same corporate face as was now used from Fiesta to D-series. The matt black finish was extended to the corner panels adjacent to the grille to give a neat and complete frontal appearance. The lower panels of the cab and the bumper, previously supplied in white, were now painted to match the upper half in one of the nine cab colour options available. Joining the two parts was a new metal strip with a less shiny, brushed aluminium finish, which now bore the model designation in addition to the 'Transcontinental' legend in a bold new script. The chrome door handles were replaced with black ones and the chrome strip from below the door glass was removed.

The inside of the cab was much as before, still providing an excellent workplace as good as any competitor, with just the replacement of the fake wood finish of the dashboard for a more classy, and restful to the eyes, slate grey.

At its launch the basic UK range comprised: 3424, 3427, 4427, 4431, 4434 in 4x2 configuration all available as HA (tractor) or H (truck-rigid) and 4427, 4431, 4434 in 6x4 configuration again as HA (tractor) and HT (truck-rigid). Production continued at the Amsterdam plant and Mk 2s would continue to roll off the Dutch line until the end of 1981. By then the Transcontinental had been propping up the huge Amsterdam plant for three years, car production having ceased in 1978, and the economics of that arrangement were untenable. Production shifted in 1982 to Foden (Sandbach Engineering), part of the US Paccar group since 1980, and continued at that factory until the end of 1983. Just over 500 examples were assembled at the Cheshire plant and despite the cost of assembly by a third party and the redirection of some key parts to a UK base, it is believed that these Transcontinentals did finally turn a profit for Ford. Speculation as to whether the last lot of vehicles were required to meet Ford's orders was rife, but most likely it was a combination of outstanding orders and Ford fulfilling contractual obligations to its major component suppliers – such as Cummins, Fuller, Rockwell and Berliet – without incurring financial penalties. In fact, it was not clear at this point that the model's fate was sealed because Ford included it in a major remarketing exercise half-way through the following year, 1983. 'Line Haul' covered the top-weight Cargos and the Transcontinental range with specific sales, service, parts and back-up facilities from 45 upgraded dealers in the UK. Unfortunately the major investment required from the dealerships to meet this standard was considerable and many dealerships that were actually good at looking after Transcontinental customers just couldn't justify the expense.

Total production figures for the Transcontinental Mk 1 and 2, equalled less than 9,000 units over the nine-year production period, a long way short of the production estimates of 580 units a month that the company had envisaged for the model in the heady days following its launch in 1975. Compared to a rival vehicle such as Volvo's F88, which produced 40,000 examples over a 12-year period, Ford's foray into heavy trucks in Europe must, unfortunately, be seen as something of a disaster. Certainly early examples suffered from weight issues, but that was largely the result of an unlucky gamble on the possibility of increased weight limits in the UK, and Ford was not alone in getting that one wrong. Early Transcontinental trucks were thirsty vehicles, but the design process was well under way before the first oil crisis of the early 1970s; if it had been re-engineered at that point, it may well not have happened at all. Both these problems were largely rectified in the Mk 2 version anyway.

The more pressing problem for operators was having to deal with a back-up and parts service that was unused to the needs and demands of premium long-distance trucks and Ford's inability to adjust from the very different practices and thinking that, conversely, made the D-series such a roaring success in the low- and mid-weight categories. It is interesting to note that those who bought the Transcontinental, from large companies to owner-drivers, and operated them for a time, found them among the best, most reliable and most economical trucks in their fleets.

Why this opinion didn't filter through to the industry as a whole in the same way as the F88's reputation, which snowballed like no other before or since, is something of a mystery. Were contented operators keen to keep the Transcontinental secret? Could Ford have marketed the range differently? What might have happened if production was UK based? Why didn't Ford hang on to see how the UK's new higher weight limit affected sales? All are questions that will never be answered and we can only speculate about what might have been. However, it must be remembered that the Transcontinental was a superb truck, being both well-designed and well-made from quality components. It was also technically advanced in some areas, particularly the sophisticated four-point cab suspension, which truly set it apart at the time and set the standard for future cab designs.

Maybe now the big Ford finally enjoys the recognition that it should have had all those years ago. One thing is for sure, if, back in the late 1970s, truck buying decisions had rested on the shoulders of 10-year-old boys, such as the author, then the amount of Transcontinentals produced would have been significantly different.

Scottish Farm Dairy Foods Ltd of Glasgow purchased these two fine HA4427 units to service a contract for Adams Foods, the Irish-owned dairy producer. The trucks performed a daily trunk to Adams' Leek depot, returning to Glasgow with full loads of dairy-based foods destined for the Scottish market. Clanford Motor of Paisley, one of the original dealers allocated to sell the Transcontinental, supplied the two units, which performed very well and were highly regarded by the drivers and management.

(Photo: Ford Motor Company)

As the revised Mk 2 Transcontinental started to come on line late in 1978, after the August changeover to the new T registration, this Mk 1 example, operated by BOC, must have been among the last of the original models to be registered. The booming North Sea Oil industry was a hungry beast in the late 1970s, and BOC's Peterhead depot was kept busy supplying it with welding and other gases. Note the substantial locker mounted under the trailer.

(Photo: Ford Motor Company)

Loads collected from Adams Foods were transhipped through SFDF's Helen Street warehouse/coldstore. From there they were delivered to customers via the smaller vehicles of the company's distribution fleet.

A third Transcontinental was added later for general fleet duties and to cover for the other two in event of a breakdown. Scottish Farm Dairy Foods, once the largest bulk supplier of milk in Scotland, went into administration in the late 1990s to be taken over by Robert Wiseman Dairies. Imagine Transcontinentals in Wiseman's black-and-white cow livery!

(Photo: Ford Motor Company)

BWB 514T, a fine example of a UK-specification drawbar outfit operated by a potato merchant, makes an impressive sight bowling down the M4. As with the Mk 1, Mk 2 rigid chassis were again designated H, or HT depending on drive configuration, while tractors remained HA whatever the layout. The 4x2 rigid chassis was available in two wheelbase options of 3.9 or 4.5 metres. This one is nicely matched to the trailer, which presents a pleasingly balanced combination. Both wheelbase options were available for operation at 34 or 44 tonnes. *(Photo: Marcus Lester)*

Removing the Ford lettering from the upper front panel on the Mk 2 cab created an ideal space for livery and sign writing, an opportunity realised by this operator. Unlike Mk 1 cabs, where the lower GFRP panels were supplied from the factory in white, Mk 2 cabs generally came in an overall colour. Ford offered five basic colours: white, grey, red, light and dark blue along with four 'fashion colours', such as Radian Yellow, which would be changed from time to time. Transcontinental cabs, unlike the rest of the commercial range, from Transit to D-series, were not offered in primer, only a full gloss finish. *(Photo: Marcus Lester)*

Cabmont International, a wholly owned subsidiary of Cables and Montague Ltd, had a country-wide haulage and warehousing operation with depots in Southampton, Bristol, London, Cambridge, Liverpool and Glasgow. This handsome Transcontinental marked a return to British machinery and was one of several operated from the company's Erith depot, which boasted an impressive 180,000 sq ft warehouse. In the 1970s, Cabmont won a lucrative contract with ACT to handle containers and tilts throughout the UK and Europe. Note the early F88 240 in the background, which clearly shows the 10-year gap in development between the two truck types.

(Photo: Ford Motor Company)

Norman Keedwell never grew his business to match the size of that of his older brother, Ray (R T Keedwell); instead he preferred to remain more or less a one-man operation. Over the years he has run some top-class trucks, including V8-engined Scanias, a Kenworth and, most recently, a heavy haulage Volvo FH. The Transcontinental followed a MAN and looked particularly good in Norman's usual light blue colour with fine panel pin-striping, every bit a match for the smart livery of his brother Ray's trucks. R T Keedwell didn't operate any Transcontinentals, but did run a Berliet TR280, MYB 576V. Note the original yellow cab colour on the door pillars. *(Photo: Marcus Lester)*

These four Transcontinentals, bearing consecutive registrations, make an impressive sight in the smart livery of own-account user Rockware Glass Ltd. Rockware established its glass-making business in Greenford, Middlesex in 1919 and by the late 1960s had, through the acquisition of various competitors, further facilities in five other locations in the UK. In 1977 the company made a pre-tax profit of £9 million and employed over 6,000 people. The Transcontinentals were part of the company's purchased fleet, which handled the transport of 30 per cent of the company's output, while hired-in vehicles handled the balance. *(Photo: Ford Motor Company)*

The drawbar concept enjoyed a surge in popularity with UK operators following a change in the law in 1972, which did away with the requirement for a driver's mate on such combinations. This H4427 with a 4.5-metre wheelbase hauled windows for a subsidiary of the Doulton group of companies based in Manchester. Although not running at the same height due to the smaller wheels of the trailer, the de-mountable van bodies were the same size and could be swapped between the truck and trailer. Combinations like this offered the operator great flexibility, but required diligent planning to give the best results.

(Photo: Ford Motor Company)

A significant handover of new trucks for Ford dealer, Hanford Motors of Oxford. This impressive four-truck line-up was half of an order for eight Transcontinentals placed by Midlands BRS in 1979. Midlands BRS, usually the operators of more 'bread and butter' machinery, had been evaluating the performance of six earlier Transcontinentals over a two-year period during which it reported virtually no faults despite the units clocking around 50,000 miles each a year. Clutch life averaged 130,000 miles and the brakes were yet to be re-lined on any of the units. The BRS trucks were HA3424s, which delivered a healthy 240 bhp via a Fuller nine-speed gearbox to perform well at 32 tons.

The Transcontinental had been designed with fleet use in mind and it was essential to break into the general UK market if the range was to be a success. Co-operation with BRS, an organisation noted for its 'tight margins' operating policy, was an ideal way to broadcast that the Transcontinental was not just a 'bells and whistles' TIR express, but a good general-purpose machine that could even turn a profit at 32 tons. That, and the fact that the BRS Transcontinentals were employed on trunking operations between Ford's Birmingham, Southampton and Basildon sites suggests that a mutually attractive deal for the eight trucks may have been struck between the two parties.

(Photo: Ford Motor Company)

Civil Engineering Company, William Tawse Ltd, was responsible for some major civil projects throughout Scotland, including the Fast Reactor Facility at Dounreay. In the 1960s, Tawse rebuilt the beach esplanade at Aberdeen and later linked Baleshare and North Uist with a 350-metre causeway. Indeed, such work had given the company an early boost when it was subcontracted by Balfour Beatty to complete a section of the Churchill Barriers at Scapa Flow during WW2.

BSS 363T was the company's prime mover. An HA 6x4 chassis, the unit was probably a 4431 (315 bhp) or 4434 (345 bhp) and almost certainly was fitted with the 13-speed Fuller gearbox to get impressive loads like this moving. *(Photo: Ford Motor Company)*

The Rigblast fleet, which also included ERFs with similar specifications to this Transcontinental, were kept busy supplying the North Sea industries of oil and gas extraction with sheet metal. They would also transport loads to any of the regular transit ports including those as far south as Lowestoft and Great Yarmouth. Continental runs were also undertaken, and, judging by the roof beacons fitted to this smart HA4427, loads could be outsized on occasions. Note the optional cab striping applied to this otherwise standard unit.

(Photo: Ford Motor Company)

Spain's own domestic heavy truck was provided by Pegaso and, rather like the Transcontinental, the range was powered by one basic engine in varying states of tune. While Ford fitted the proven Cummins 14-litre NTE series, Pegaso used its own design with exotic, Hispano-Suiza heritage. The Spanish manufacturer also specified Fuller transmissions, and, if it were not for strict government control on domestic content, would probably have used Rockwell axles too. The Pegaso product was a strong and competent performer, but its European back-up was no match for that of Ford. Maybe that is why this Spanish operator chose the Transcontinental for its international work, although the Ford logos on the trailer suggest a link with the manufacturer may have had influence. (Photo: Ford Motor Company)

Beavis Plant's Transcontinental makes an impressive sight with this Poclain excavator onboard as it goes about its business. Although sporting a black Mk 2 door handle and crossover T registration, this unit was actually a very late Mk 1 with original door trim strips (without model designation), FORD lettering (although re-located to the main grille) and chrome strips on the bottom of the door windows. Note that the lower steps, which were bumper mounted, have been removed from this unit, probably to give better ground clearance at the front when delivering plant like this to off-road locations and building sites. (Photo: Marcus Lester)

It would seem the driver of this interesting example has repositioned his two remaining windscreen wipers further around their splined shafts so as to still cover most of the screen, possibly as a running repair or maybe in preference to the sweep pattern of the original three-blade layout. Note the air-conditioning unit, not of the type offered by Ford, fitted to this mildly customised unit and also the rather unusual extra flaps mounted ahead of the landing legs of the trailer.

(Photo: Marcus Lester)

Sadly, with the introduction of the sliding bogie skeletal trailer, the dedicated 'short skelly' for handling single 20-foot containers such as this has almost been consigned to the history books. The author always liked the look of a premium tractor unit with this type of trailer/load and this fine HA4427 with its anonymous livery is just such a case. Aesthetically the Transcontinental's height seems to work very well with the container load to create a very purposeful-looking combination.

(Photo: Marcus Lester)

With even the most modestly equipped HA4427 6x4 chassis tipping the scales at over eight tons (nearer nine for the more powerful variants), heavy haulage and plant movement was the only sensible application for such units employed on UK-only work in the days of the 32-ton limit. The goalposts in the UK were moved in 1983 with the introduction of the limit of 38 tonnes on five axles, but the trend by then, if choosing three axles for the unit, would have favoured an un-powered tag axle, or similar, giving the capacity increase, but without the weight penalty or drag of a 6x4 layout.

L C Lewis's magnificent heavy haulage Transcontinental was powered by the big NTE 370 Cummins and worked alongside a 4x2 example that handled lighter plant movements and general haulage. The two Fords spurred a succession of Cummins/Fuller powered trucks from Foden and Scammell. Note the missing cab trim strips on the offside. *(Photo: Marcus Lester)*

Factory white with optional cab striping was the basis of this plain, neat and simple livery for Hayward Freight. NWL 886T, an HA4427, is seen at two stages of its life while parked up at Cavendish Square in Swindon. Hayward's work included contracts with Norfolk line and Ferrymasters. One of the latter's part-stripped tilts is seen here. Note the Mk 1 chrome door handle fitted to the nearside.

To satisfy the regulations of all the countries to which the Transcontinental was available, it was necessary for Ford to accommodate certain changeability within the basic specification. One such feature was the reflector strip behind the front indicator in the bumper. Some countries required a side marker light in this position and if fitted it replaced the UK market reflector with a lens and bulb. Side marker bulbs were easily changed via a quick-release lamp holder behind the bumper, unlike the indicators in front, which required the Mk 1 Granada assembly to be unscrewed and removed first. *(Photos: Adrian Cypher)*

The late John F Jossaume poses proudly – while awaiting a police escort on the M180 out of Hull – with his second Transcontinental and a Priestman VC15, weighing around 16 tons, loaded on the unit's dedicated Tasker trailer. LVX 937V, equipped with a Cummins 290 and 13-speed Fuller, was ex-Ford PR fleet and was put up for sale with just a few hundred kilometres on the clock, possibly following a TV appearance. This unit replaced Jossaume's earlier vehicle, JAR 56N, which was one of the original demonstration fleet sold by Ford in November 1975. JAR 56N was a 4x2 HA3424 unit with a 3.07-metre (121-inch) wheelbase with the larger capacity, but normally aspirated, 15.18-litre engine producing 252 bhp, Fuller nine-speed box and a 4.11 final drive ratio, a specification which made it something of a flying machine! Jossaume, now run by John (Jnr), sold LVX 937V in 1988 following a long career moving plant. The replacement was a day cab ERF E-series. Note that the Priestman's tracks are parked at right angles to the trailer as this actually presented the narrower width. (Photo: John Jossaume)

This nicely presented unit with GAP tilt was registered just two numbers away from Jossaume's LVX 937V, yet was operated by a South Wales operator on the other side of the country. Could it be that this top-weight HA4435 was also an ex-PR fleet vehicle? Ford's PR and demo trucks would often be festooned with extras from the SVO (Special Vehicle Orders) list. Demonstration trucks in particular, would almost always feature the third crew seat for example, so the light grilles fitted here could be further evidence of a past in PR.

(Photo: David Wakefield)

Ford's ever-active PR team struck a major coup when they agreed a deal to supply the cars and other vehicles required for the fast-paced television action series, The Professionals. The series, expertly created by Brian Clemens and Laurie Johnson, started in 1977 originally with British Leyland supplying the cars, but reliability issues and a lack of understanding from BL as to what was required in terms of continuity soon opened the door to Ford and its slick PR department. The series not only made stars of the lead characters, but also boosted the profile of the Escort, Capri and Granada with its weekly slot on primetime television. Of course, when the script called for a truck, Ford's PR team were only too happy to help. NWC 67V appeared in two episodes 'A Man Called Quinn' and 'The Gun'. Another unit, KVM 210V, enjoyed star status as the subject of the title in the episode, 'Hijack'. NWC 67V is seen here in the employ of a fictitious pharmaceutical company during filming of a sequence for 'The Gun'. In between takes, Martin Shaw, who played Doyle in the series, is seen trying out the truck. (Photos: Ford Motor Company)

This interesting rigid chassis was employed on own-account work for MSE Scientific Instruments, which was part of the Fisons Group. As the designation is that of an H3424, the lowest weight/engine combination, it is feasible that the truck operated as a solo rigid and not a drawbar, especially as it was obviously despatched abroad under TIR carnets where distances and conditions would have made more sense of a 240-bhp 16-tonner! FNJ 574V was featured, again as a solo rigid, in the 1980 Transcontinental brochure. This may have been because the work it was involved in was interesting, but perhaps it suggested to potential buyers that the Transcontinental could also be considered for the role of distribution truck, though maybe not for multi-drop work! *(Photo: Adrian Cypher)*

Not a 1979 unit as the V registration suggests but an updated pre-1978 example as evidenced by the early style grille and original side script without model designation. Perhaps not registered for some reason until 1979, this unit was more likely imported, which, given its LHD layout, seems to make sense. Given the incestuous and metamorphic nature of motorsport, it is entirely possible that the whole unit and trailer combination started out with another European team before running in the colours of the alloy wheel manufacturer, ATS (Auto Technisches Spezialzubehör). Whatever the circumstance of its registration, it certainly made a handsome transport for the German team, which operated in F1 from 1977 to 1984. Despite employing the services of top-name drivers like Jochen Mass, Keke Rosberg and Jan Lammers, ATS's inauspicious F1 career netted just seven constructor's points, no pole positions and no wins. However, in 1981 it did nurture Slim Borgudd, the ex-ABBA drummer, who went on to be a top truck racer.

(Photo: David Wakefield)

Ian Walker of Haynes Ford supplied Ken Trowell with all his Transcontinentals over the years. Thanks to Ian's enthusiasm and Ken's chequebook, all enjoyed a degree of customising. For example, GKR 633V gained a vertical exhaust system, polished alloy diesel tank, air horns, sun visor and light grilles. Under Ian's direction, Haynes' workshop developed and fabricated its own mounting system for vertical stacks on the Transcontinental and Ian also oversaw the first installation of a night heater to a RHD example. The bulk of Ken's work was hauling concrete castings for companies like Milton Pipes Ltd of Sittingbourne. *(Photos: Ian Walker, Ford Motor Company)*

A few years later, the GKR 633V returns home via Dover following a rare trip across the water with a flatbed trailer, probably having delivered Milton concrete products to Europe. Still looking tidy, the unit has lost its headlight grilles, the mirrors have been replaced with wider items and the wheels have been given a coat of white paint and gained step rings. There is also evidence of a repair to the main grille in the bottom right corner, the grille catches were located here and the area could become brittle with age and prone to damage. Note the driver's proud celebration of his truck's Cummins engine, in this case a 274 bhp example, which he's mounted below the Ford badge.

(Photo: David Wakefield)

NWC 56V was the fourth Transcontinental to be pitted against the cream of the day's premium tractor units in Truck magazine's gruelling Eurotest series. The HA4432 unit ran in the 1980 contest and was up against some first-class machines from DAF, ERF and Fiat. The Cummins NTE 350 fitted in the unit was a slightly de-tuned version of the range-topping engine and was good for 315 bhp and nearly 1,000 lb-ft of torque at a lowly 1,300 rpm. Ford's engineers opted for a tall back end, using the 3.70 ratio. The resulting performance was astonishing, placing the HA4432 as the third fastest truck around the route since the first test in 1975. But somewhat more importantly, it was also the second most economical truck ever, finishing just behind DAF's fuel miser 2800 DKSE. This was a big feather in the caps of both Ford and Cummins, proving that the new NTE engines could not only deliver the power and performance of the old NTC range, but could also now compete on fuel consumption with established market leaders like DAF. NWC 56V is seen on the continent with the test's Savoyard trailer in tow. *(Photo: Ford Motor Company)*

NWC 56V, without number plate and back on PR duties, poses with a Crane Fruehauf tilt, probably on Tilbury docks, a favourite Ford location. The LHD layout would have been chosen specifically for Truck magazine's Eurotest, indeed, the unit was typical European spec with the longer 3.5-metre wheelbase allowing for the common 1.6-metre continental kingpin setting and a 400-litre diesel tank. Eurotest contenders could carry any available option listed by the manufacturer and the roof spoiler was one that Ford offered on the Transcontinental range. Although only beneficial at constant motorway speeds its inclusion in the specification no doubt aided the overall mpg result achieved by NWC 56V. Even though the Mk 2 Transcontinental had shed a good deal of weight, Ford still sent this example out to do battle with the competition lavishly equipped with the extra crew seat, double bunk and window blanks. Despite these extras it weighed in just below 7.3 tons, only beaten on that score by the super slim Fiat at 7.1 tons.

(Photo: Ford Motor Company)

Steve Murty pioneered truck racing in the UK, first putting on the spectacle at his New York Dragway, Yorkshire in August 1978. Racing followed the American blueprint with a pair of tractor units racing head to head over a standing quarter-mile run. Although the contestants were standard working trucks, they were, back then, un-governed. Run times were impressive with trucks taking 21–24 seconds to cover the measured distance at speeds of over 60 mph. Buoyed by the success of the early meetings, Steve decided to up the ante and, with sponsorship from Bandag and the generous assistance of Ford, which included the use of a PR fleet Transcontinental, the Bullet was born. Based on a humble D1314 tipper chassis, the Bullet used a highly modified version of Ford's six-litre engine, originally developed by Sabre Marine for powerboat racing, which was prepared by Ford racing guru, Terry Drury. With turbocharging and intercooling it initially produced 300 bhp (rising to around 400 with later developments) at 3,400 rpm. There was also a prototype, six-speed gearbox and Eaton two-speed rear axle. The four-ton machine was capable of 108 mph and held the class record for the standing quarter-mile at 18.2 seconds and 71 mph. (Photos: Steve Murty)

The HA4435 Transcontinental with 3.5-metre wheelbase came from the Ford PR fleet as part of the deal and was painted, by Ford, in the smart, matching Bandag colours, while Crane Fruehauf provided the trailer. Note Steve's appropriate private plate, which was transferred to the truck while in his care. As well as providing stylish traction for the Bullet, the Transcontinental found its way onto the strip too, where Steve would demonstrate the truck's capabilities in this dramatic fashion. Washing up liquid and gentle brake application while under power was enough to break traction before Steve would drive it up through the gears while stationary in a tyre-melting display of the big Cummins' torque. Luckily, Bandag's sponsorship included a ready supply of re-mould tyres for both the Transcontinental and the Bullet. Note the repositioned Ford badge.

(Photos: Steve Murty)

Due to Ford policy, Steve's original Transcontinental was returned for disposal after 12 months to be replaced by OWC 818V, which Ford also painted in the dramatic Bandag colours. The new HA4435 tractor was virtually identical apart from the larger capacity diesel tank and slightly different Bandag logos on the doors. Two more un-liveried examples were also provided before the Bullet project was wound up.

Steve followed the Bullet with the Pirelli Project. Based on a Ford Cargo, the new truck used a 24,000-bhp Rolls Royce Avon 302 jet engine from a Lightning fighter in a specially modified chassis to give a 200-mph capability. (Photo: Steve Murty)

NWC 74V was another of Ford's PR fleet Transcontinentals, this time loaned to the Road Haulage Association for use with their travelling road show, the Compact Campaign, which was built into the matching trailer. The Compact acronym stood for Conservation of Oil Maximum Productivity and Competitive Transport. In keeping with the last part of that acronym, this unit, along with the Bandag-liveried OWC 818V, took part in the 1980 Beaujolais race, each hauling 1,200 cases of the wine in an attempt to be the first commercial load back to London from Beaune, France. In the event the gaudy pair missed the necessary ferry connection out of Boulogne – OWC 818V, with the bigger engine, by just 20 minutes and the 315-bhp NWC 74V, another 30 minutes behind that.

(Photos: Ford Motor Company)

Even in its slimmed-down Mk 2 state, the 6x4 Transcontinental chassis, offering sub 20-ton payloads as it did, was an unusual choice for operators at the UK's 32-ton limit. Being as this example was an HA4427, with the 274-bhp version of the NTE 290 engine, perhaps overall weight was not the main operating concern, but rather the danger of drive-axle overloads caused by the unusual netted load carried here. Note how visible the chassis components were behind the grille if painted in a light colour such as this yellow. *(Photo: Ford Motor Company)*

In contrast, this 4x2 HA3424, with a design GCW of 34 tonnes, represents the other end of the scale and was very much the entry-level model of the Mk 2 Transcontinental range. With 240 bhp and 840 lb-ft of torque, it was adequate for most UK applications at the time, especially those under the maximum weight. For those wanting the lower-weight chassis, but who operated over hilly ground or long trunk routes it was perhaps better to opt for the HA3427, which offered the same chassis but utilised the 274-bhp version of the same engine. Note the customised roller blinds fitted to this example. *(Photo: Marcus Lester)*

Two later examples of Rockware's Transcontinental fleet registered on V plates. Ford, in a concerted effort to bring in fleet sales, offered the Ford Operating Cost Analysis System, or FOCAS. This elaborate, for the time, computer-based system could provide operators with detailed reports on a monthly or quarterly basis giving breakdown costs per mile of the entire fleet or individual vehicles. It was also able to give comparisons between Transcontinentals and other makes of truck operated within the fleet. *(Photo: Ford Motor Company)*

With such a big canvas available, there were various options open to the operator when applying a livery to the Mk 2 Transcontinental. The author's personal preference was always for the retention of the factory-black grille and lower corner panels, but some operators did choose to paint these items. The scheme on this example, where only the corner panels and main bars of the grille have been painted, seems to work better than a complete covering of paint as applied to the Rockware vehicle.

(Photo: Ford Motor Company)

The 4x2 HA4427 chassis was perhaps the most ideal for UK operators. The model was ideally suited to 32-ton operation and offered a great balance of economy and performance. As the NTE 290 was essentially the same 14-litre unit as the higher powered versions at the top of the range, it was very under stressed at 274 bhp and thus proved hugely reliable, and not just for Ford, as it was also popular with competitors such as ERF and Seddon Atkinson. Frozen distribution was the perfect role for the HA4427 and Unispeed, parent company of Birds Eye, rated the Ford very highly, running more examples than any other UK operator. Indeed, fleet numbers often exceeded 100 Transcontinentals at a time. This was just the sort of operator that Ford had envisaged for the truck, but sadly was in the minority. (Photo: Ford Motor Company)

The Transcontinental was fairly unique among heavy trucks in that the front hubs were lubricated with oil rather than grease. The system was utilised to give greater service life as the oil started to work immediately, unlike grease, which needed to reach its operating temperature first. The front axle beam was an 'I' section forging with capacities between 6,500 and 7,500 kg and came from the top-weight D-series trucks; one of only three components on the entire truck to come from Ford's extensive European parts bin. Note the external air supply connector just below the bumper and just to the left of the step loop. This was a frequently fitted option on the Transcontinental. Routed forward from the air tanks, it was easily accessible and allowed the air system to be charged from another source in the event of a compressor failure, or run from a recovery vehicle while under tow. *(Photo: Ford Motor Company)*

The basic back axle choices offered for the Transcontinental were Rockwell's tried and tested R170 and R180 items with capacities of 10 tonnes and 11.5 tonnes respectively. Both were fully floating and featured single-speed reduction. For those wanting higher capacity from a 4x2 set-up, there was also the U180 axle available, which, via a special heat treatment process, was capable of higher weights up to 13 tonnes. The axles used opposed taper bearings to resist side loadings. Given the nature of bulker work, the chances are that the operator of this HA4427 opted for the higher capacity R180.

(Photo: Marcus Lester)

This smart example operated by Taunton Meats worked alongside trucks from Fiat, Mercedes, Magirus-Deutz and Volvo, specifically the F88. Ford developed the Transcontinental when the F88 was very much the benchmark truck for long-distance work; however, the F88 design was 10 years older, making the Transcontinental more comparable to the later F10 and F12, such was the Ford's superiority over the earlier Volvo, particularly in terms of driver comfort. The pilot of this example would have enjoyed far more roomy and comfortable accommodation than any F88 driver. (Photo: Marcus Lester)

With the generous size of the windscreen it was necessary for Berliet to provide the cab with a three-wiper system to give the necessary coverage. On the Transcontinental a single 24-volt Lucas motor drove the three 500-mm blades via a neat system of linkages and splines located behind the upper opening panel on the front of the cab. As the wipers were not of the wet type, three fixed nozzles at the base of the windscreen provided cleaning fluid instead. Since the wipers would self-park at the bottom of the screen, it must be assumed that the ignition was cut mid-sweep in this instance. Note how close the registration of this example is to that of the M R Pearce unit on the previous page. (Photo: Marcus Lester)

Toleman's superb HA4432 F2 racing car transporter was at the cutting edge of aerodynamic developments for heavy trucks in 1980. The unit featured an elaborate, one-piece roof spoiler with side skirts, an under-bumper fairing and enclosed chassis sides.

Rather less obvious, but also geared to fuel efficiency, was the prototype Pirelli tubeless tyres on which the truck ran. A deal struck with Pirelli allowed the tyre manufacturer to closely monitor the performance of its LS91 tyres over real conditions.

Toleman's F1 team (1981–1984) was privately owned and eventually became the hugely successful Benetton. Along the way it launched the careers of Derek Warwick and Ayrton Senna as well as numerous 'behind the scenes' people. *(Photo: Ford Motor Company)*

The interior sun visors of the Transcontinental were roller blind type, which ran on guides at the edge of the screen and a central guide loop. The lowest position covered almost half of the windscreen's depth. The blinds remained at the height they had been pulled down to and they would return to the top position only when a release lever in the centre was pulled. Because it was necessary to have the loop support in the centre, the two-piece system left an unfortunate gap through which the sun could penetrate, so, for the Long Haul Cab, Ford provided a separate small sun visor of conventional fold down design for the centre. *(Photo: Marcus Lester)*

The distinctive three-slot vent in the front upper panel, slightly damaged on the example in this picture, fed fresh air directly to the main heater and vent system behind. The Transcontinental was fitted with a powerful two-speed fan system for screen demisting and general air circulation around the big cab.

This 1980 vehicle must have been working well within its design capacity with this rather interesting, top-loading, single-axle van trailer. Loads were, presumably, high cube rather than high weight. Note the large air deflector, which is nicely matched to the trailer height. *(Photo: Marcus Lester)*

C & S Motors' H4427-based wrecker was a state-of-the-art machine back in 1980, equipped as it was with a Heeco, twin-ram underlift. The Transcontinental worked alongside a Scania LBT141, fitted with more traditional Holmes 750 lifting gear, from C & S Motors' North London base in Bowes Road. While the Ford with 100 bhp less could not match the big Swede for power, its high-tech gear was much quicker and easier to use for conventional breakdown recoveries. Note the extended bumper mounting, required to accommodate the front winch, which gave the added benefit of moving some useful weight forward as a counter balance for heavy rear loadings. *(Photo: Ford Motor Company)*

Although wearing a V registration, it is unlikely that this unit was actually a post-1978 Mk 2 example because it has been fitted with Mk 1 chrome door handles, and early door trim strips without model identification. However, not being left-hand drive, it is also unlikely to have been an import registered in the year that it came to the UK. Although not in the original position, the correct Ford lettering is also present and a blue oval badge has been fitted, higher than normal, to the main grille. Possibly a late registration of an early example, or a truck re-registered having been seized following default of payments and/or legal proceedings. Whichever it was, the Ford made a handsome truck for this operator.

(Photos: Marcus Lester)

A precarious load of pallets makes up the load for this smart Transcontinental as it barrels down the M4 during a hot summer in the mid-1980s. The glass fibre reinforced plastic bumper of the Transcontinental was, unfortunately, prone to accidental damage, particularly on the exposed corners. The bumpers of other trucks would often bear witness of a knock to the corner in the form of a kink further back, but the Transcontinental was likely to lose the end portion instead. More often than not, a Transcontinental would lose the indicator assembly too, as on this example. Luckily, UK-market Transcontinentals were fitted with an indicator repeater on the corner panel above. (Photo: Marcus Lester)

A well-worked Transcontinental and trailer combination, operated by Westfield International, bears further evidence, in the form of an unfinished repair, to the susceptibility of the GFRP bumper to damage. The nearside was particularly vulnerable, as the driver had no way of seeing it, while manoeuvring in tight situations. Note that the roof vents at the top of the windscreen have been removed from this unit.

(Photo: Marcus Lester)

This fine drawbar combination was one of six operated by Multiple Fruit Supplies on contract to Littlewoods Food Stores. The prime movers were all H3424s with 4x2 chassis, while the trailers were all 24-foot single-axle types running on York dolly converters. The dolly arrangement allowed the trailers to be handled by the fleet's tractor units, too. The drawbar outfits almost exclusively worked as night trunkers and performed the task admirably, 240 bhp and 13 gears proving perfectly capable of hauling 32-ton gross, even over the Woodhead Pass.

Chris Webb joined the company in 1979 and was sent out as a passenger with a senior driver to learn the ropes. The truck was a demo Transcontinental artic unit and trailer. Unfortunately, the senior man could not get to grips with the Fuller gearbox – the fleet was 95 per cent Scania at the time. In the end, Chris, a Leyland Marathon veteran, had to take over.

The H3424s were disposed of in 1982 and replaced with Scania 82Ms. The power drop was noticed by the drivers; Woodhead Pass was a far slower climb.

DWB 225V was fleet number 158 and was equipped with an early radiotelephone. *(Photo: Chris Webb)*

The windscreen washer system was fed from a four-litre reservoir located behind the front bumper via a pump mounted next to the right-hand headlights. Topping up the reservoir, which could be emptied by the pump at a rate of 1.14 litres a minute, was achieved by lifting the lower grille to reveal the filler cap on the top of the reservoir. In the event of a pump failure, the GFRP bumper would first have to be removed (a relatively simple six-bolt operation) to gain access to the pump's mounting position on the face of the front chassis cross member.

(Photo: Marcus Lester)

The author was thrilled to locate this photograph in Ford's archives because, as an impressionable 13-year-old boy, he spent many happy hours gazing at this image of NWC 67V and studying the features and details of the unit. The photograph originally appeared in the large-format book Super Trucks by Nick Baldwin, published in 1981, and was just one of many featuring the truck and trailer that were taken during a photo shoot at Tilbury Docks. The resulting photographs cropped up in all sorts of publicity material for Ford and the Transcontinental. At the wheel is Maurice Richardson, the lucky man charged with delivering Ford's test fleet and PR trucks to journalists throughout Europe. (Photo: Ford Motor Company)

Despite the towering 3.2-metre height of the cab, the Transcontinental always looked beautifully in proportion. This was largely due to a greater portion of the cab being ahead of the axle centre line and the impression of slimness given by the comparatively narrow – when compared to the doors – sleeper windows. The handsome cab profile, here enhanced by optional window blanking plates, and tidy chassis layout all added up to make the Transcontinental an impressive-looking truck. This example, part of the PR/demo fleet has numerous options including; cab striping, chassis catwalk, coupling lamp, spare wheel carrier and transverse exhaust system. This last item was designed for tanker applications and utilised a single silencer system mounted transversely under the clutch housing, which exited forward rather than aft of the airtanks. Note the new, pre-delivery Transits in the background. *(Photo: Ford Motor Company)*

Another view of the same HA4432 unit shows the spare wheel carrier installation on the offside, which has dictated the fitment of the smaller 300-litre (65-gallon) diesel tank. The same spare wheel carrier could also be fitted on the other side behind the battery box, while a different version was available for mounting on the rear cross member. Both types featured a wind-down winch mechanism. This unit is pictured earning its keep during a European trip to deliver a left-hand drive PR department Cargo for road testing by a magazine. Note the 'on loan' low loader trailer provided by Crane Fruehauf, a company with which Ford enjoyed a close working relationship. (Photo: Ford Motor Company)

Early in 1981, Truck magazine was granted special dispensation by the ministry to run a 38-tonne artic on UK roads for demonstration purposes. The Armitage Report was suggesting 38 tonnes as the new domestic limit and at the time there was no hotter subject in UK haulage. Having recently run a Transcontinental through the magazine's Eurotest at 38 tonnes, Ford was the manufacturer approached to provide a similar spec HA4432 unit for the comparison test. Luckily for Truck, Ford had a near identical unit in NWC 67V and was only too happy to loan it, complete with this superb Euro-spec road/rail tilt, to prove its worth on UK roads at 38 tonnes. At this point Ford fitted the unit with a roof spoiler to give the very best mpg figures during the test. Truck's findings were published in the March 1981 issue of the magazine and suggested that operators could look forward to increased productivity of around 18 per cent for a 38-tonne truck that spent most of its time on motorways. (Photo: Ford Motor Company)

Actor and comedian Rowan Atkinson's passion for all things automotive, especially fast cars, also extended to trucks. Rowan memorably drove the Leyland T45 tipper used in the 'Not the Nine O'clock News' music video for the song 'I Like Trucking', a parody of life on the road with an emphasis on squashing hedgehogs. Since Rowan holds an HGV licence he was in the unique position of being able to drive the truck for his touring comedy show. An approach to Ford led to the loan of this impressive, top-spec 6x4 HA4432 – a priceless photo opportunity for the PR department. *(Photo: Ford Motor Company)*

A well-worked Transcontinental with an after-market tag axle. Ford only offered a tag axle as an SVO option, meaning that the main production line only produced 4x2 and 6x4 chassis. The favoured item came from York and was an air-suspended fulcrum type. Depending on the legislation of the country of operation the axle was fitted with twin wheels on York grease-filled hubs, or single wheels on Transcontinental front-oil-filled hubs, if the latter, the wheel would often be fitted with the Transcontinental's distinct step ring/trim to mirror the front. York hubs featured 'S' cam brakes, while the Ford hubs retained the standard wedge system. Note the missing middle wiper, sagging offside bumper and extensive aerodynamic aids. The Transcontinental went out of production before major developments in aerodynamics were mainstreamed, so the vehicle was only offered by Ford with the fairly rudimentary roof spoiler arrangements of the day. Whether or not it enhances the Transcontinental's looks, the considerable effort that has been applied to bring this one up to 1990s standards has to be admired. (Photo: David Wakefield)

Frequent trips to sunnier climes have taken their toll on the once smart paintwork of this HA4428 unit operated by Curries. The HA4428 was a direct replacement for the HA4427 and was introduced over the 1979–1980 model year. The new model was little changed, but did register a small increase in engine power when rated in PS rather than bhp or KWs. Curries' continental services were supported by two European depots, which aided turnaround and virtually eliminated empty running.

(Photo: David Wakefield)

The Welsh National Opera's fifth and final Transcontinental was HWO 620W, an HA4428 unit finished in the new WNO livery of white and burgundy. By 1980–1981, four Berliet/Renault TR280s had replaced all the company's earlier Mk 1 Transcontinentals. Although on a W registration, it was actually slightly older than the Renaults, having been pre-registered with a V plate and held in the WNO's storage facility until required. The Ford's job was as the dedicated orchestra truck, fittingly the most prestigious role, and was piloted by husband-and-wife team, Mark and Kate Terrell, while the four French trucks handled scenery and props. The TR280s were part of a sponsorship deal with Renault, but the trucks failed to impress the WNO drivers with their inferior steering lock, which hampered access in the typically tight city centre locations of many venues and were noted for their smoky engines and idiosyncratic gearboxes. The Renaults were kept for six to seven years, but the Transcontinental managed eleven before replacement, which by then was provided by Mercedes-Benz.

HWO 620W is seen parked outside the theatre in Wiesbaden and in an image taken by Kate, on a rudimentary camera, while she stood next to Truck's reporter, Philip Llewellin, as he photographed the two trucks as the subject of his 'Long Distance Diary' story for the magazine in July 1982. (Photos: Mark & Kate Terrell)

JMG 269W was probably one of the best known and highest spec Transcontinental drawbar outfits to be operated by a British company. The impressive H4435 6x4 prime mover and trailer combination ran out of North London during the early 1980s in the livery of European Freightbus. Normal work was groupage loads destined for the continent with produce, usually picked up in the Low Countries on the return. The drawbar layout gave good flexibility for split loads and offered certain economies over an articulated alternative on the same work. Note the large 600-litre diesel tank and natty wheel trims – very 1970s! *(Photo: Ford Motor Company)*

JMG 269W descends into Dover on another European trip. Now devoid of any reference to Freightbus, the truck and trailer look somewhat plain and just a little tired, but still no less imposing. A number of LB Scanias also operated under the European Freightbus livery, including V8-engined 140 and 141 types. On paper JMG 269W stacked up well against the 14-litre Scanias, offering similar performance and a far superior cab and ride; however, by 1980 Scania's excellent series 2 was just around the corner and was equipped with a superb new cab that would more than redress the balance. However, Ford could not come close to matching the earlier Swedish product in terms of back-up and spares availability. This shortcoming would cost the Transcontinental dearly, stretching the patience of even its most ardent supporters.

(Photo: David Wakefield)

The Fuller gearboxes fitted to the Transcontinental offered three power take-off facilities, the third of which was driven by an extended auxiliary counter shaft. The third drive was standard on the 13-speed gearbox, but had to be specified as an option on the nine-speed. For PTO operation, an 'All Speed Engine Control' could also be specified to allow very fine adjustment to engine speed. The control for this was mounted next to the heater slides and comprised a twist lock 'T' handle and a vernier control knob for fine adjustment. The 'All Speed Engine Control' worked in conjunction with the main PTO control knob on the dash. *(Photo: Ford Motor Company)*

Ryder's UK operation, which grew out of its acquisition of Fisher Renwick in 1973, proved a successful venture for the American giant, which was running thousands of trucks on rental and contract hire from over 30 UK locations by the mid-1980s. Following the same purchasing model as the US division, Ryder UK would, in the autumn, invite favoured manufacturers to stay at a hotel, at its own expense, and, over the course of a week, would place all its orders for the forthcoming year – often over 1,500 trucks. Ford would have supplied far more Cargos than Transcontinentals to Ryder, but this example looks particularly fine in the familiar yellow-and-black livery. *(Photo: Marcus Lester)*

With a registration just five digits away from that of the Ryder Transcontinental, could this example, seen tramping down the M4 on a hot summer's day, have started out in the hire fleet, too?

The Transcontinental was fitted with a viscous, thermostatically controlled fan by Behr. The benefits of this design – which only operated as and when required – over a fixed alternative were: a faster warm-up, lower noise levels and improved economy. Engine drain was minimal at just 10 bhp when engaged. In the event of a fan failure, the blades could be locked into continuous use by a bolt until a replacement could be fitted. Further efficiency could be gained by fitting the optional radiator shutter. This automatic, air-operated accessory would mount in front of the radiator and offer very precise regulation of the airflow.

(Photo: Marcus Lester)

This much-travelled HA4428 makes an impressive sight, even when parked up for the night, with its magnificent TIR tilt. Cab privacy in the Transcontinental, when off duty, was restricted to the bunk area as the big Ford was only fitted with curtains for the rear windows and, to form a division, between the seats and bunks. While this arrangement made for a cosy berth in which to kip, it left the vast living area in the front of the cab unavailable, unless modified, as on this example, where the driver has installed a track and added a home-made set of curtains to cover the front glass area, too. Note the non-standard diesel tank. *(Photo: Marcus Lester)*

The Brabham F1 team's HA4432 unit and trailer returns from the continent in the early 1980s. Parmalat was the Italian equivalent of the Milk Marketing Board in the UK and entered Formula 1 sponsorship in the late 1970s with Brabham, the connection being the Alfa-Romeo engines used by the team at the time. A change of engine supplier in the early 1980s saw Ford DFV power plants installed for a short time before a switch to BMW; however, Parmalat remained onboard through these changes. The Transcontinental replaced an earlier Volvo F88 as the prime mover for the team's main transporter. A full load, even with extensive spares on board, would have been around 10 tons, a weight which could have been handled with ease by a truck with half of this Transcontinental's 315 bhp, but with far less style. Note the rather neat under-bumper air dam, which is very similar in design to that of the Toleman transporter (page 99). *(Photo: David Wakefield)*

Lou Thurgood enjoyed good and reliable service from his 1976 ex-Brain Transcontinental, but by 1981 was looking for a replacement for the five-year-old vehicle. He took the plunge and ordered a brand-new one from his local Ford Dealer, Haynes Trucks in Maidstone. Haynes' salesman, and enthusiastic Transcontinental champion, Ian Walker, closed the deal and did much to influence the mild customising of the truck, including the metal flake paint, which had become something of a speciality for the dealership. The HA4428 was ordered when the 32-ton limit was still in force, but Lou continued to work it at 38 tonnes after the increase in 1983, choosing to change his twin-axle trailer for a tri-axle rather than alter the unit with a tag conversion. Lou's work was mostly groupage loads to Scotland and paper in and out of the Kent mills. The NTE 290 was sometimes a little stretched at 38 tonnes, but was a reliable performer and regularly returned seven mpg. By the time TKO 960X was due for replacement the Transcontinental was out of production, but Lou found his favoured Cummins and Fuller combination in an impressive 6x4 Foden. TKO 960X is pictured tipping amidst the tenements of Glasgow in 1983 and moving a Munro trailer, a rare event, over a short distance in Essex.

(Photos: Lou Thurgood)

Before being delivered to its new owner, TKO 960X, as yet unregistered and with incomplete livery, was earmarked by Ian Walker for some special, high-profile promotional activity for a garage equipment manufacturer. Following an initial enquiry from Tecalemit of Plymouth, Haynes delivered the Transcontinental, along with a Cortina saloon, to Olympia for the 1981 show where the truck was posed, dramatically, atop one of the company's four-post lifts. Note that TKO 960X was supplied as a fully glazed cab with the glass painted over, rather than being fitted with the optional window-blanking plates, as is evidenced by the, as yet, unpainted window rubbers.

Ian Walker considered the Transcontinental to be a remarkably good truck and was extremely proactive in its promotion. Indeed, he alone was responsible for selling the type at Haynes because the management, believing Ford should stick to the mid-weight categories, wanted little to do with it. Ian started his remarkable 50-year career with the Kent dealership as an apprentice and covered every aspect of the business before settling into truck sales.

(Photos: Ian Walker, Tecalemit)

Another of Ken Trowell's mildly customised Transcontinentals emerges back into England via Dover following a continental trip. Ken started as an owner-driver in 1972 and he bought his first Transcontinental in 1979 as a replacement for his Leyland Marathon.

As a great admirer of American trucks, Ken favoured the Cummins/Fuller/Rockwell layout and considered the Transcontinental's cab to be the best available at the time, affording unparalleled views of the road.

As the Transcontinental was equipped with a high-capacity cooling system, it is doubtful that Ken's grille-blanking modifications caused any problems with overheating. The smoothed airflow may have even have had a positive effect on mpg figures. (Photo: David Wakefield)

Germany, with its very strong Ford connections, proved a good market for the Transcontinental, particularly in the drawbar sector. With a range tailored towards the higher output variants and, to some extent, rigid chassis for drawbar use, it was also unusual in that it offered a 6x2 layout as a mainline product, which it listed in brochures and spec sheets, rather than as an option. However, German 6x2s were supplied the same way via SVO post-production, but it was interesting that it was marketed very differently to this particular country.

The distinctive stripe decal, introduced in 1978, featured three shades of one colour – blue, green or red – or as a mixed version of blue, red and brown. As a standard option it gave scope for operators to create a distinctive-looking truck without breaking the bank. *(Photo: Ford Motor Company)*

As the Transcontinental's chassis and running gear were so robust and durable, it was generally the cab that would show the first signs of age and ultimately let the truck down; early examples were particularly prone to rust. Luckily for operators, Renault continued to use the cab for its own heavy range until 1992, long after Transcontinental production ceased, and as the cab was essentially the same it was possible to swap them. The key difference was that from 1977 the Berliet/Renault version featured a raised centre floor section to clear the new and taller MDR 635 engine and a revised cab-lock mechanism. Ford had refused to change to cabs with these modifications so Renault, for an additional fee, continued to provide the original spec version for the Transcontinental. There were also some minor differences to the A and B pillars below the waistline, but these were easily modified and the correct Ford lower panels could be fitted, as on this example. Other detail differences include slightly larger running lights above the screen, no top screen vents (on later examples) and a roof hatch (again on later examples).

This conversion, which has retained its Renault badge, also features the French machine's dashboard. Renault launched a revised R310 in 1982 and at that point introduced a new higher dashboard, which continued across the width of the cab at the same height.
(Photo: Clive Davis)

The author must declare a personal interest here as MHY 370Y was driven by his brother-in-law, Terry Bright, and was the only Transcontinental he ever rode in as a boy. Terry moved to Janes from R T Keedwell, where he was driving a Seddon Atkinson 401, also with a Cummins/Fuller driveline, in the early 1980s and took over the big Ford as his regular drive. The truck, although registered in the UK on a 1981 Y plate, was actually a much older LHD Mk 1 example, which had started out life on Dutch roads. The truck was fitted with the original NTC 14-litre engine in the highest state of tune, which meant 340 bhp and a spirited performance at 32 tons. The towering height and soft cab suspension of the truck meant that it was not considered to be an obvious choice for racing, but its output was encouraging enough for the owners to enter it in the UK's first circuit race for trucks at Donnington in 1984. Running in the up-to-350-bhp class, the truck, co-driven by Terry, put in a credible performance considering its size, age and handling issues. MHY 370Y is seen unloading at the Vidal Sassoon warehouse in Saffron Walden and the Colman's factory in Norwich. (Photos: Patrick Dyer)

A neat tag-axle conversion allowed this smart, owner-operated Transcontinental to maximise the tax break by running a three-plus-three-axle combination at 38 tonnes while providing traction for the Dutch concern, Detrafor, in the UK. Detrafor changed its name to Continental Carriers in the early 1990s, at which point the trailer colour changed from blue to red, this one probably representing the changeover period. Note the truck's replacement bumper and the addition of FORD lettering to the panel above the grille.

(Photo: Adrian Cypher)

Maurice Richardson's job as delivery driver for Ford's press trucks took him all over Europe and would inevitably lead him to pay visits to many of the company's factories. It was on one such trip to Germany that he encountered this HA4432 unit parked up and awaiting disposal. The truck had spent much of its time hauling Ford prototypes around in a box trailer, hence its plain and anonymous livery, and was now surplus to requirements. Maurice made an offer and bought the unit, returning with it later to the UK on trade plates. Note the long wheelbase, spare wheel carrier mounted on the rear and chock location behind the battery box. *(Photos: Maurice Richardson)*

As it had led a sheltered existence and had always been well maintained, Maurice's Transcontinental required only a light restoration, as well as UK-type approval and registration before becoming a show truck. Here the finished article lines up with a Cargo cousin. In 1983, Ford remarketed the Transcontinental along with the top-weight Cargo under the 'Line Haul' banner. This saw a marked improvement in specialised service for these trucks from 45 upgraded UK dealerships. There were also minor spec changes including a 460-litre diesel tank. The remarketing was thorough with eight-page advertisements in the leading magazines and dedicated 'Line Haul' brochures. The whole process could not have been cheap, which begs the question: Were Ford considering keeping the Transcontinental in production as late as 1983?

Although the Cargo range eventually topped out with the 40-tonne 4028, it was never going to replace the Transcontinental as a premium long-haul truck because its cab just didn't have the room or driver appeal. The difference is highlighted clearly in this comparison shot.

(Photo: Maurice Richardson)

While the Sierra, the rear-drive replacement for the much-loved Cortina, was just emerging in the autumn of 1982, the Transcontinental was unfortunately entering its twilight years with final production having transferred to Foden's Sandbach plant in Cheshire for the last push. However, PR opportunities – like this shot for Emerson Envelopes – still arose and were put to good use promoting both the car and truck range. The Sierra range represented a huge investment for Ford and proved a massive success that spanned 11 years before replacement. Experts at the time estimated that a new truck range would cost in the region of £200 million to develop plus around £150 million for a new plant to produce it. Little wonder then, that Ford, with fingers burnt from its first European heavy truck foray, canned the Transcontinental without a replacement programme. *(Photo: Ford Motor Company)*

Courtney Transport's superb Transcontinental makes an impressive sight as it punches down the M4 in full 38-tonne guise. The Portsmouth-based company also ran a Leyland Marathon, itself a reasonably high-profile truck thanks to its cut-and-shut version of the Ergomatic cab, which usually served Leyland's middle-weight trucks. Unlike the Transcontinental, the Marathon range did not extend beyond the 290-bhp threshold, but between 240 and 290 bhp it offered similar performance and generally higher payloads on account of its lighter weight, even in full sleeper form. However, comfort and appointment were not in the same league. *(Photo: Marcus Lester)*

While this Transcontinental is a highly impressive example, it seems much modified with a 6x2 back end not of Ford origin, judging by the unfamiliar hub assembly of the drive axle. There are also changes to the battery box and air tanks and a DAF under-bumper air dam has been added. The engine, according to the badge on the grille, is an E14 from Cummins, a type that was not available until well after Transcontinental production had finished. Given the extensive modifications made elsewhere, however, it is entirely feasible that this type of engine was fitted under the cab. BLJ 28A is seen loading an excavator at Hydrex's facility in Charlton. *(Photo: Adrian Cypher)*

This machine is almost certainly one of the Sandbach-assembled units that represented the last 500 or so Transcontinentals that were built. NTS 537Y was one of five run by George McLaughlin. George started his haulage business in 1976 and as an ex-Ford truck salesman for Frews of Perth, it was little wonder he chose Transcontinentals for his top-weight tractors. The HA4432 had ample power, even for long trunking operations south with full 38-tonne loads. Today, George's fleet comprises smart Volvo FHs in stunning red, white and blue livery. *(Photo: John W Henderson)*

One way to get onto a blocked pump! Ford's Maurice Richardson brims his tank while en route delivering a test fleet Cargo to eager journalists on the continent in the early 1980s. Although swapping tank locations was common enough on other trucks, the high-tensile steel frame of the Transcontinental made the practice extremely difficult and highly inadvisable. Maurice was responsible for all aspects of his trips, including the booking of hotel rooms, as he rarely slept in the cab, and secure parking for the truck and load, the latter often being a valuable pre-production example of a new model. Although he could often have driven the test vehicles directly to their destinations, Maurice usually opted to use an artic to transport them, which greatly reduced the chance of damage. Note the replacement mirrors on the Transcontinental. *(Photo: Ford Motor Company)*

Although not fitted to this particular unit, the Transcontinental was available throughout its life with a clever headlight wash/wipe system for the main, outboard headlamps. Dictated by the deep recess mounting in the bumper, the system drove a curved blade in 180-degree sweeps around the lamp via a motor and gearbox while cleaning fluid was delivered. The driver controlled the process of cleaning by depressing a spring-loaded switch on the dashboard. While this switch was depressed, it would illuminate until the wipers cycled once and then extinguish as long as the wipers had parked in the correct place and no other failure had occurred. (Photo: Ford Motor Company)

A LHD-spec 6x4 HA4435 with all the feel of a Middle East unit, complete as it is with air conditioning, double-skin roof and a sturdy fridge trailer with wide spread axles. Although not very obvious, this unit is also fitted with corner deflectors to divert spray away from the side windows and mirrors. Fouling of these items in bad weather was not a marked problem for the Transcontinental, unlike the Berliet/Renault, which, especially in its early days, was notable for the problem. Perhaps, the raised height of the cab when fitted to the Ford chassis made all the difference.

(Photo: Ford Motor Company)

With its towering height, the Transcontinental was, perhaps, not an obvious choice as the basis for a vehicle transporter. However, Silcock and Colling invested heavily in this specialist drawbar design, which was already proven on its earlier ERF B-series trucks. The prime mover was based on a short 4x2 rigid chassis fitted with a small-diameter wheel tag axle. Despite its height, the Transcontinental offered a straightforward profile for the body designer with a vertical back panel that was devoid of any intake plumbing and a nice flat roof, without even a roof hatch to consider. Silcock and Colling operated a number of Transcontinentals with this layout, which, almost exclusively, hauled new Cargos, four at a time, out of Ford's Langley plant. Silcock and Colling were later merged with old rivals, Toleman, under Tibbett and Britten's Axial Logistics banner. *(Photo: Marcus Lester)*

Jean Rondeau was a noted French racing driver who, following early forays in single seaters, settled on a successful career in sports car racing. Rondeau produced his own cars with Ford DFV engines and it was in one of these that he won the Le Mans 24-hour race in 1980, the only person ever to win in a car of their own manufacture. Rondeau was based near Le Mans and was tragically killed in a road accident a few years after his historic victory. Quite why this Transcontinental, in the livery of a UK paper manufacturer, is hauling the Rondeau racing transporter back towards France is unclear; maybe it was between owners at the time. G R Macmillan later became Connaught Macmillan before dissolving in 1989. *(Photo: David Wakefield)*

In 1984 Ford put together the 'Techline Tour', a mobile exhibition created for the benefit of Ford's workforce, which toured its factories throughout Europe. The exhibition was contained in custom-built semi-trailers that joined together on site to provide a walk-through experience showing just how 'great' Ford was and what a privilege it was to be employed by the automotive giant. Inflatable skirts and portals disguised the trailers' working bits and pieces while the interior design leaned heavily on Sci-Fi TV programmes of the era. Edwin Shirley Trucking handled the logistics and provided the drivers, but the famed EST livery was nowhere to be seen as Ford provided smart, matching, silver HA4432 units for traction.

(Photos: Imagination Europe Ltd)

Ford disposed of the Techline Tour Transcontinentals, probably through the usual Frog Island outlet, as soon as the tour was finished. The HA4432 units were barely broken in and made excellent purchases for anyone on continental traffic, specified as they were with left-hand drive and the longer 3.5-metre (138-inch) wheelbase, which was more suited to European kingpin settings. This fine example was snapped up by an Irish operator and re-registered. Note the chassis locker, an option only made possible by the longer wheelbase. (Photo: David Wakefield)

With his passion for the Transcontinental unabated, Ken Trowell ordered one of the last as his own fleet flagship. The truck's spec befitting its role being fitted with the NTE 370, the highest rated Cummins available in the Transcontinental range, and a sturdy 6x4 chassis. The truck also featured numerous extras, mild customising and special paint, all of which bumped up its price to a wallet-wrenching £44,000 – although with discounts the final figure was nearer £36,000. Ken proudly takes the keys from Ian Walker and the late Frank Wood of Haynes. Frank was the Sales Manager prior to Ian and completed fifty years with the company. Between them, the two men served a staggering 100 years of service with Haynes.

(Photo: Ian Walker)

Somewhat later on, and with some obvious miles under its wheels, Ken's flagship HA4435 takes a break while waiting to load in Scotland. Ken's development of the truck has been ongoing, and at this point the unit features a massive chrome bumper and bull bar, though the latter had also been briefly attached to the original Ford bumper before replacement. Gone are the one-piece rear wings, replaced by half-guards with roll-out tops and the interior has been re-trimmed and a US-style steering wheel installed, too. Ken, heavily influenced by the American scene, cited the big US Ford CL9000 as his ideal truck. A949 MKK was among the last hundred or so examples to be assembled by Foden Engineering at the end of the truck's eight-year production life. *(Photo: John W Henderson)*

The white-painted grille of this smart 1983 HA4432 clearly shows the vertical centre strip, which seemed to disappear from post 1978 Transcontinentals. In fact, the grille design did not change from Mk 1 to Mk 2, but the 'corporate' matt black finish applied at the changeover disguised this fact so well that most people assumed it was a new design. Show-Haul were based in Kent and jumped on the concert tour bandwagon – forgive the pun – in the early 1980s and served its contracts with the typical step-frame box vans favoured by that industry for ease of loading and to accommodate the high-cube equipment carried. *(Photo: David Wakefield)*

The wonderfully named Pig Improvement Company employed the services of a number of Transcontinentals, both units and drawbar combinations, from its two UK bases. Solo running without trailers was not uncommon for the drawbars, but with the valuable loads and the big Fords often returning 10 mpg, the trucks still earned a good profit delivering throughout Europe. Note the chasing ERF C-series. The C-series offered similar Cummins/Fuller/Rockwell specifications to the Transcontinental, especially in CP (Common Parts) guise, but it never shed the 'gaffers' motor reputation of previous ERFs, a tag with which the aspirational Transcontinental never had to contend. (Photo: David Wakefield)

A nice example, working on produce deliveries in and out of the London markets in the late 1980s.

Transcontinental production shifted from the Amsterdam plant to Foden Engineering early in 1982 and finished for good at the end of 1983 when Foden shut down for the Christmas break. It is believed that the UK production, which amounted to just over 500 trucks, fulfilled Ford's outstanding order and contractual requirements for the model. Foden's skilled workforce was more accustomed to bespoke trucks assembled under the Paccar banner, so Transcontinental production, though repetitive, was simple and represented useful revenue for the Sandbach site during difficult times for the industry.

(Photo: David Wakefield)

A covert image of two recently completed Transcontinental tractor units awaiting pre-delivery inspection at the Sandbach plant in 1983. Foden assembled both left- and right-hand drive vehicles from 1982 to 1983. Colour choice was no longer an available option with all cabs painted plain white and shipped complete from Berliet/Renault, much as they had been back at the start of production in 1975. This saved the time and the cost of kit assembly as had become the practice at Amsterdam. To further streamline production, Ford, when asked for a cab without rear glazing, would no longer fit cover plates to a cab with window apertures, an SVO option back in Amsterdam, but would instead order one from Renault without the apertures cut out. Most of Renault's own production was supplied in this manner anyway.

(Photo: Adrian Cypher)

This fine pair operated by a Dorset haulier provides us with the perfect parting shot. Very late registered on B registrations, they must have been among the last of the Sandbach-produced vehicles to be put on the road in the UK, although rumours of C and D registered examples persist. One at least, features a tag-axle conversion and both have Mk 1 FORD lettering added to the grilles. Interestingly, B841 WPP is fitted with a Mk 1 trim strip, without model designation, on the door, while B655 XGS has a door trim strip that is completely devoid of the Transcontinental script. Note the external grille catches fitted to B655 XGS.

(Photo: Marcus Lester)

LET IT LUG!

Best Cruising Speed Range

Working Speed Range

Caution

12 · 14 · 16 · 18 · 10 · 20 · 8 · 22 · 6 · 24 · 4 · 26

For peak performance and economy, your Cummins E series and NT240/NT250 engines will work best if you follow the green colour band gear change pattern. Engine speed can lug down to 1200-1300 rpm before a downchange.

Change down late - Change up early.

Cummins

The dash sticker that accompanied the new NTE engines made its point clearly and drivers had to ignore the time-honoured tradition of using instinct – derived from the tone and feel of the motor – to change gear and instead use the rev counter and allow the engine speed to drop to unnaturally low levels, for the time, before changing down. The NTE engines of the Mk 2 Transcontinental were class-leading and did much to rectify the hard-drinking reputation of the Mk 1.